Priya and Sanjay Tandon

PRABHAT
PRAKASHAN

Published by
PRABHAT PRAKASHAN PVT. LTD.
4/19 Asaf Ali Road,
New Delhi-110 002 (INDIA)
e-mail: prabhatbooks@gmail.com

ISBN 978-93-5186-826-2
SUNRAYS FOR FRIDAY
by Priya and Sanjay Tandon

Edition
2025

Price
₹ 400.00 (Rupees Four Hundred only)

Sketches, Art Work and Painting on the Cover by
Priya S. Tandon

Printed at
Narula Printers, Delhi

Dear Reader,
God loves you!
Realize this truth!

A collection of stories compiled and presented with love on 23.11.2015, the 90th Birthday of our Beloved Bhagwan Sri Sathya Sai Baba

ॐ

राष्ट्रीय स्वयंसेवक संघ

प्रधान कार्यालय – डॉ हेडगेवार भवन, महाल, नागपुर 440 032
email - hedgewarbhavan@rediffmail.com

तिथि : मार्गशीर्ष पूर्णिमा, यु. 5117 दिनांक : 25.12.2015

Parables, i.e. simple short stories are the best medium to convey the ideas effectively. Human being from all walks of life, from all age groups, from all economical groups and of various intellectual acumen can be reached by the appeal of the parables and they effect humanity deeply. Therefore everybody in the world who wanted to appeal to the heart of humanity to awaken values and wisdom in them has used this medium of parables.

Sri Sanjay Tandon has been sending a one line good thought to about 2,500 people on email everyday for the last 15 years. Inspired and encouraged by the response they made these emails into books namely Sunrays for Monday, Tuesday and so on. His inspiration behind this is spiritual and hence the proceeds from the sale of the books are used for charitable service purpose.

The present volume "Sunrays for Friday" is a sixth in the series. I am sure the simple stories and the thoughts expressed by them will help awaken a value based conduct in the readers and thus will render our life and present world a notch beautiful.

I congratulate Sri Sanjay Tandon and Smt. Priya Tandon for this noble endeavor and wish the series all success.

(MOHAN BHAGWAT)

Dedication

Dedicated to our Beloved Bhagwan Baba ...
who is the air we breathe,
the thoughts we think,
the smile on our lips,
the light in the darkness and
the love in our hearts.

Priya and Sanjay Tandon

The manuscript of this book was offered for blessings at the Mahasamadhi of Bhagwan Sri Sathya Sai Baba at Puttaparthi on his 90th birthday, 23.11.2015.

Prayer

The consecration and consummation of the human mind,
The connotation and calibration of the written word!

As it flowed from you to us, Dear Lord,
Collected in this book is only your word!

Born in your likeness, Oh Beloved Lord,
We strive for that finesse, Oh Bountiful Lord!

Bless us to work for you as you please,
Nothing shall put us more at ease!

This work is yours, to bless and share,
Infused with your love, grace and care!

-Priya and Sanjay Tandon

February 10. 2016

FOREWORD

A saint was walking along a street where he observed three sculptors, each working on a slab of marble, slowly chipping away at the slab. The saint enquired with the first sculptor what he was doing, the first sculptor replied that he was feeling very depressed and felt unfortunate that he had to work under the hot sun and hammer away at these un-forgiven and harsh stones,. On asking the same question to the next sculptor, the second sculptor responded that he was fortunate to have some work and by doing so, he was earning a living and could feed his family. The saint then turned to the third sculptor, who was deeply engrossed in his sculpting and only when he had finished his work and was satisfied with it did he turn to the saint and very humbly with folded hands said that he was blessed to have been given the opportunity to create a marvel which would be worshipped by millions for ages to come!.

The reason I have narrated this story is that this is the feeling I derive when I read any edition of Sunrays. What Sunrays does is it chips away the unwanted layers of ego, desire, greed etc. and veritably brings forth the truth... It chips away the unreal to reveal the real!

Start each day of the year with reading and reflecting on Swami's quotes or reading one story and you will find that these minute moments of transformation culminate into a mega transformation .

Sunrays provides the most fertile seeds for children. All that each parent or teacher has to do is to provide water and manure of being ideal. This will not only help the child to imbibe the greatest lessons in human values and spiritual thinking through an age-appropriate methodology but will also help the parents and teachers in their own growth.

I pray to Swami to bless this divine effort .

Yours In His Service,

(NIMISH PANDYA)
All India President
Sri Sathya Sai Seva Organisations
India

Jagdish Singh Khehar
Judge
Supreme Court of India

6, Moti Lal Nehru Marg,
New Delhi - 110011

FOREWORD

I came in touch with Priya and her elder sister-Madhu when they were students, at the Department of Laws in the Panjab University at Chandigarh. And through them with Hon'ble Mr Justice M. M. Punchhi, who adorned the Office of the Chief Justice of India. My first impression about Priya and Madhu was, that they had been groomed and raised with traditional values, which we Indians cherish and are proud of.

I attended their weddings, and came in contact with Sanjay-Priya's husband, and Pawan-Madhu's husband. Sanjay is the son of Shri Balramji Dass Tandon, a household name of political stalwarts in north India. He is presently the serving Governor of the State of Chhattisgarh. It was a surprise that Sanjay, who belonged to a political family, had also been brought up, so as to be possessed of sacrosanct traditional Hindu values.

Having seen them over the years and the way they brought up their children, one could visualize a very important role played by their mothers – Brijpal Tandon and Meera Punchhi. Both Sanjay and Priya have remained steadfast in their cultural values in that, they sent their children to Puttaparthi for schooling, at the feet of their Guru-the revered Bhagwan Sri SatyaSai Baba.

Through the Sunrays series, they have made a conscious effort to share their values with the world. Their sixth book - Sunrays for Friday, is a powerful expression of their understanding of faith and devotion. The stories narrated by them contain simple hidden messages. The sketches made by Priya would enable the reader(s) to visualize the projection. But more importantly, in sharing their values through this sixth in the Sunrays series, they have practically made the highest offering at the feet of their Guru- Bhagwan Sri SatyaSai Baba.

My best wishes to Priya and Sanjay Tandon. The Sunrays series which started with Sunday has covered Monday, Tuesday, Wednesday, Thursday and Friday. I hope, readers will not have to wait too long for Saturday.

Jagdish Singh

(JAGDISH SINGH KHEHAR)

NEW DELHI;
FEBRUARY 09, 2016

after the morning session at the Mandir, I bumped into Dr. B. Prabha, a gynecologist at the General Hospital in PrashantiNilayam. She said to me, "I have been looking for you Priya, I have an old book of stories called Chandrakant. It is in hindi. I want to give it to you, because I think you are the person who can best put it to good use." I was a little taken aback, for I just know her a little. Her grandson was Satyam's class mate. I said, "Auntie that is very sweet of you. I would love to go through it." So I went along with her to her apartment and she gave me the book with utmost love. She carefully packed it in a neat polythene bag and handed it over to me saying, "You have inspired so many people through your books. Whenever I see this book on my shelf, I think of you. Now that I have been able to give it to you, I feel I have done my bit." The love and grace with which she gave it to me, made me say, "Auntie, you are giving this book to me, but I feel that Swami is giving it to me." And she said, "Of course Swami is giving it to you! Don't you see? He wanted you to have it. So He inspired me to give it to you. That is how He operates. He does not physically do everything for anyone. He gets things done by putting the thought into someone's mind!" I was at a dearth for words then; but through the medium of words, and His inspiration needless to say, a number of stories from it, have found their way into Sunrays forFriday. Truly, man proposes; God disposes!

All of us go through phases in life; sometimes good, and sometimes bad. It is our attitude that sees us through rough times.When floods come, fish eat ants. But when floods recede, ants eat fish. Time is the key player. God gives opportunity to everyone. May we have the good sense to understand that we don't have to just go through life; we have to grow through it too ...

After Swami's leaving His body, the onus of carrying forward His mission of love and peace is on those whom He loved most. As He once said, "To those whom much is given, much shall be asked...." Well, it is payback time now; we have been amongst the favoured few, so how can we possibly shirk the responsibility of participating in the furtherance of His work! His work is now our work! Swami, we know that when you have assigned the work to us, you will find the ways and means to push it through. We are reminded of a song that I(Priya) learnt as a teenager, while attending Swami's ten day Residential Winter course on Spirituality at Delhi.

This is how it goes ...

Why fear when I am here,
So said Baba, Sathya Sai Baba,
Sathya Sai Baba My Lord!
Why fear when I am here ...
All I want is your love my child,
All I want is your faith,
All I want is your love in God,
No matter what is your faith!
So said Baba, Sathya Sai Baba,
Sathya Sai Baba My Lord!
Why fear when I am here ...
Krishna, Buddha, Jesus, Allah
All came to this land,
All of them brought a message of love,
Love your fellow men.
So said Baba, Sathya Sai Baba,
Sathya Sai Baba, My Lord!
Why fear when I am here ...
The light you see in the dark of night
Is that of God and man,
Find the light that is in your heart
And reach the Promised Land.
So said Baba, Sathya Sai Baba,
Sathya Sai Baba, My Lord!
Why fear when I am here ...

So, when the Master of the Universe is the Captain of our ship, why should we have fear of anything? Our Lord has given us the joy of

Preface

OM SRI SAI RAM

Everything they say happens only when it is destined to happen. Despite earnest intentions of compiling this set of stories into Sunrays for Friday, we have taken an unduly long time to do so. Worldly reasons and excuses one side; the will of God is the primary reason.

Swami's physical absence in Puttaparthi, is painful and there is nothing; absolutely nothing that can compare with the bliss of having had His darshan and Divine proximity. Now, all we have is memories of those beautiful moments of love and bliss. But there is something new in Puttaparthi. A feeling that was not there before! What is that? The computer science teacher at the boy's school, Mr. V. Prusthy put it very simply, when we asked him how people were managing without Swami being physically present. He said, "Everything goes on as before. Earlier Swami was in one place. He was either in the Mandir or in the school or at His residence ... Now, He is everywhere! Now everyone has his own Swami! Swami is with everyone!"

What a profound thought! Said so easily; so smoothly; but what a deep connotation it had! The form had passed on into the formless! The finite had dissolved into the infinite! The physical had permeated into the metaphysical! Swami is everywhere! Show us a place where He is not! The beautiful memory of what Swami had said to us in a personal interview in 2001, came flooding back in an instant. He had said, "I am in you, with you, around you, besides you ... I am always with you!" With those words He had taken our breaths away! Surely life is not just about breathing. It revels on moments that take our breath away! And then it dawned on me ... let us not regret that He has left us; let us rejoice that He came to us, just for us and He shall live on through us and in us till eternity!

The unsullied truth is that He is always with us and He is always with you ... With each one of you! What is important is whether you can feel Him or not. He is like perfume, once the perfume has been sprayed; you can only feel it or smell it ... You cannot touch it or see it. If you can take Swami's hand and walk with Him all day long; if you can think of Him as you walk, you will find that all traits in you, that you want to get rid of in yourself, will gradually fade away without any pertinent efforts from you. They cannot survive in the light of the Lord. They will fade away and die.

We remember once attending a program by a theatre group performing Raas-leela. The scene was one where all the Gopikas were dancing around Krishna. They were so engrossed in His thoughts and in such bliss, that each one of them felt that Krishna was dancing with her and her alone. This was beautifully portrayed on stage by ten young boys, each dressed as Krishna, dancing with ten Gopikas. Each one had coupled with a gopi, and each couple danced in bliss. By the end of it, all the Krishnas left the stage except one, who was playing the lead role. Didn't God say, "I am one ... I will be many..." That is something only God can do!

God is everywhere. He is so small that He is present in the atomic particle. At the same time, He is so large that He permeates into the entire cosmos. He is the inexhaustible energy around us all.

Swami is our life breath, without Him we cannot even breathe! We are ... because He is! We are what we are ... because He is what He is!

I(Priya) had visited Puttaparthi in the last week of March 2013. Our youngest son Satyam was studying in Class XI then in the Sri Sathya Sai Higher Secondary School at Puttaparthi. During my stay there, one day as I was musing to myself, I said, "Swami, how will the next book get made? I don't have enough good stories yet." The same day, bringing up three sons. Our eldest son, Saraansh, is an Engineer in Computer Science. He is making software. He floated his own software company by the name of 'Competent Groove.' As his Guru Dakshina to His Lord, the first and second Apps he made, when he started his work were called 'Sunrays,' and 'Sai Vahini.' These applications are available for Android phones to receive a motivational message every day and an inspirational story every Sunday. These are available on the "Google Play Store" and are free of cost. What can one possibly offer to the Supreme Lord as Guru-dakshina? But in his own small way, Saraansh made this gesture and did us proud!

Even as we write this, Swami says, 'Why are you proud? He is mine; he is my child, and you are only the gardeners who are tending to the flowers growing in my garden. You are just the caretakers!"

Yes Swami! Our children are yours! In all humility we thank you for giving them to us, to love and nurture! Our responsibilities towards the children have found a new dimension, with our eldest son Saraansh getting married to Umang. Incidentally, Swami came in Saraansh's dream and gave permission and blessings for his wedding. And in this new relation with the new member in our home, our guiding light is something Swami once said in a discourse, "Be a mother/ father-in-love, to your daughter-in-love!"

Our second son Shiven's connection with Swami is so strong that sometimes when he says something, we feel that Swami Himself is speaking! He has read the script of this book and meticulously given some very valuable inputs to improve and bring it to this shape.

Satyam, our youngest son, after completing class XII in Swami's school at Puttaparthi is now studying Law. He is writing some amazing poetry too. While he was studying in PrashantiNilayam as he would sit in front of Swami's Samadhi, his pen would start to glide ... and he would create magic!

Swami! Please keep our children on the right path and guide them and guard them to live the kind of life, we are trying to throw light on, by this series of books.

Swami left His mortal coil on the 24th of April, 2011. My (Priya) mother was then battling against Cancer. Swami gave her some magnificent, beautiful and divine experiences in delirium wherein she understood that Swami was getting ready to put an end to His sojourn on Earth. After He passed on, my mother lost the will to live. She finally merged into her beloved Swami in August 2011. Her devotion and direction in life knew only Swami and she loved Him with all her heart and soul. She was truly Meera who loved her Sai Krishna dearly! My father Justice Madan Mohan Punchhi (former Chief Justice of India), too merged into Bhagwan Baba in June 2015.

Even otherwise this period has been very hectic in our personal lives. I (Sanjay) have been shouldering the responsibility of President BJP, Chandigarh for a second term now. My father, Sh. B. D. Tandon was appointed Governor of Chattisgarh State. Our eldest son got married in January 2015. With so much happening, we have perhaps not given our due share of time to Swami's mission, to which we have been closely connected and blessedly so! For this we offer our apologies to our Beloved Bhagwan and pray to Him to bless this offering of love as He has so graciously blessed all the earlier ones.

A lot of work has gone into the making of these books. But what really matters is the resultant effect caused. I have lost track of the number of letters, messages and Emails we have received, telling us that these books have helped them to better themselves as human beings. In this age of smart communication, we need to focus now on what is termed as SMN by The Radio Sai team at Puttaparthi. They said, "SMN is our abbreviation for a string of three Sanskrit words that Swami uses sometimes. They are: Sravanam, Mananam, and Nidhidyasanam, meaning respectively: Listening, recalling and digesting. What Swami means is wise words must first be heard, they must then be recalled and reflected upon. Thereafter, the meaning of what one has heard must be absorbed, digested and internalized for subsequent use as circumstances might demand."

The Aaj Samaj Newpaper has been publishing one story from our book every week for over a year. With this book being done, there is only one to go before we complete the Sunrays for all the days of the week. Sometimes we sit back and think; what next? The answer is not immediately forthcoming, but one thing we are sure of, that is, that Swami will continue to give us something or the other to keep us connected to His mission. There will always be something to keep us occupied and our thoughts, words and deeds focused on the teachings of our Beloved Bhagwan. He is our Divine father, our very own, and He cannot forsake us. Thank you Swami, for the constant assurance that we live in your heart as you live in ours! Thank you for being a part of our lives and for making us a part of your life... a part of your sojourn on Earth!

With utmost love and devotion, we present this offering of love at the Lotus feet of our Beloved Swami. Prayerful Pranams and Salutations to Him who is the indweller of our hearts!

He is the one ...

... who inspires,
who directs,
who prompts,
who executes,
who encourages,
who admonishes,
who applauds,
and also basks in the glory of success!!!

Priya and Sanjay Tandon

Moving ahead with Digitisation

We have been sending a one liner good thought from the discourses of Bhagwan Baba to about 2500 people every day for the last fifteen years. In this age of Digitisation and Social media, our son has made two Apps to widen the reach of these daily Good thoughts.

Sunrays and Sai Vahini are two mobile Apps available on the Google Play Store and Apple App Store for free. These are developed by Competent Groove and contain all the data of good thoughts and stories available in the Sunrays series of books.

Competent Groove has also released the ebooks for all the Sunrays books and they are available on all the major ebook stores. You can get them at http://sunrays.tandonindia.com

Connect with us on Facebook at http://facebook.com/sunraysbooks

Sunrays and Sai Vahini also post a good thought daily on facebook at the following pages:
http://facebook.com/sunraysapp
http://facebook.com/saivahiniapp

Acknowledgements

How does one acknowledge the Lord for all His bounties? There are no words to offer justification for all that He has blessed us with or offer gratitude for the bounties He has bestowed upon us. All said and done, what more can we say but this, 'We are ... because He is! We are what we are ... because He is what He is!'

It is imperative on our part to acknowledge:

Mr Anchal Singh Jamwal	For his devotion to this project and his ever willing attitude in punching in our hand-written notes
Our friends and family	For their encouragement and love for this project which is so dear to our hearts
Our Parents: Smt. Brijpal Tandon & Sh. BalramjiDass Tandon (Governor of Chattisgarh) Late Mrs. Meera Punchhi & Late Justice Madan Mohan Punchhi (Former Chief Justice of India)	For the life lessons they have taught us and shared with us to light up the pathway for us

Our Children:	
Saraansh & his wife Umang Shiven and Satyam	For their faith in us and their involvement in each little detail of this work that is so precious to us
Prabhat Prakashan	For taking up the task of publishing this book
Kapil Dev Khanna and Prachi Saini of Chandika Press Pvt. Ltd.	For their support and help in preparing the manuscript in such little time and for taking care of all the little details too
All our Readers	For all the words of appreciation and encouragement over the years

Thank you Swami, for keeping us bound together through the ups and downs of life. For helping us to understand that we have to sacrifice our personal time and comforts, if we want to do our bit to make the world a mite better! Together we stand not as 1 and 1 to make 2, but with your grace we stand together as 1 and 1 with the strength of 11.

Jai Sai Ram!

Priya and Sanjay Tandon

Contents

1

The History of Mankind

"Start this spiritual discipline as early as possible in life, do not postpone it any further. For, no one knows when the span of life will be brought to a close."

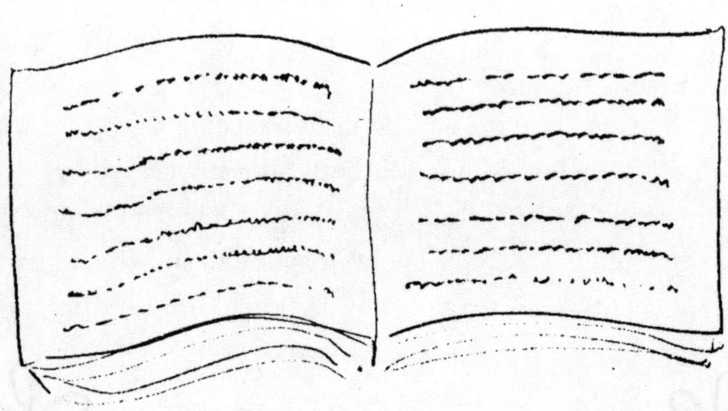

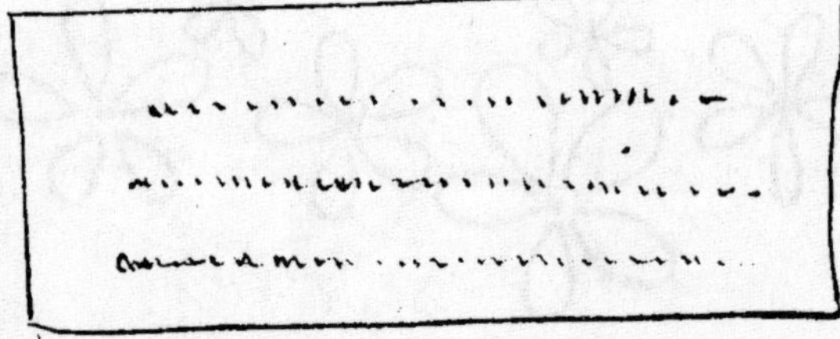

In ancient times there was a king who wanted to know everything about the 'History of mankind'. He appointed a scholar in his court, to write a book on the said subject, for the king to read. The King also named a team of juniors who would assist him in the research to be done for writing the book. The scholar worked tirelessly for years before he was able to compile a huge volume to be presented to the king. With much fanfare, the book was brought to the king's court and unveiled by the king. The king gave it one look and said, "Oh! This is a huge text. I am extremely busy in the discharge of my duties as a king. How do you expect me to read this enormous text? Take it away and give me a concise version that I can read."

The scholar took the book back. He worked on it for years together, till finally, he was able to prune the text to make an easily understandable, concise version, taking care to put in all the important facts and figures.

When the king saw the new book, he exclaimed, "What is this? This doesn't seem to be significantly shortened! It seems you have been idling away your time. How on Earth do you think, I have the time to read this Tome? If I were to start reading this, who shall look after the affairs of the kingdom? Why don't you understand? Make it shorter, my friend!"

The dejected scholar lowered his eyes and picked the book up. He spent the next couple of years again, in further cutting and pruning the text. Finally he was able to produce a thin book. He was very pleased with himself and he was sure he would please the king too.

The king opened the book and said, "Uh! Uh! What small handwriting! How can I possibly read this with my weakened eyesight? Anyways, it's still too long. Summarise it further. I am a king. I have no time for frivolous pastimes. This book will take up much more time than I can afford to spare."

The scholar was at a loss for words. The book contained merely a few tens of pages. How could he possibly encapsulate the history of mankind into something even more concise than this? Well! He had no option but to start all over again and further refine his work.

Years passed. The scholar returned with his work. It was a single sheet of paper that he presented before the king. The king had become old by now. He said, "My friend, you seem to have summarised it well this time. But I am an old man now and my eyesight is just not the same. I am afraid I shall not be able to read it now. Will you be kind enough to read it aloud for me?"

The scholar bowed before the king and cleared his throat. He read:
'Man is born in this world.'
'For some time he stays here.'
'Then he dies!'

That is the story of mankind! Three sentences are all it took, to tell the story. Birth and death are common to all. How we fill up the intermittent years, depends upon us or on our karma!

2

Just Kill All the Oldies

"Even if the standard of life is poor, it does not matter if the way of life is pure, full of love, humility, fear of sin and reverence towards elders."

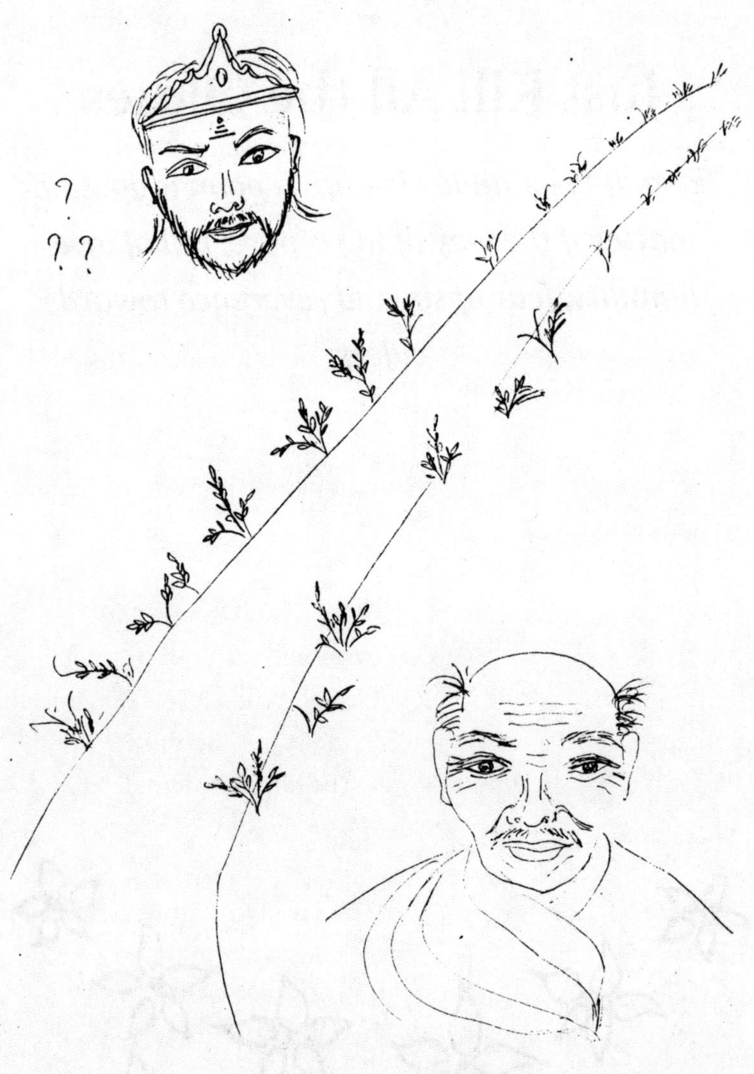

A young king was facing shortage of food in his kingdom. At the advice of his young ministers, they decided to kill all the old men and women in the kingdom. The king passed the orders, "Just kill all the oldies. The number of mouths to feed shall become considerably less and the food shall become sufficient for all." So the king's men scanned the entire Kingdom and killed all the oldies i.e. all the people who were above sixty five years.

In the kingdom was a young fellow who loved and revered his father a lot. So, before the king's men came, he hid his father in a large vessel containing wheat. He secretly looked after his father.

All the other oldies were killed and with them were lost their wisdom, experience and good sense.

The following year, there were no rains and the famine worsened. Now even the youngsters and children started dying of hunger for there was no food to eat. When it was time to sow the crops, there were no seeds in the stores, because everything had been eaten away. The kingdom was deep in despair.

The young fellow, who had secretly saved his father, discussed the problem with him. The father said, "Till the soil on all the road sides." The young fellow got a group of friends together and they ploughed the road sides. Soon, there were tiny sprouts along the road sides. The saplings were transferred to the fields and they had a reasonably good crop. This was reported to the king. The king questioned the man. He wanted to know how this had happened. The young man said, "I don't know. I had secretly saved my father against your orders. Perhaps it is because of his blessings."

The old man was brought before the king and questioned. He said simply, "Every year the farmers carry their grains in carts to the marketplace for sale. Some fall out of the carts and get deposited by the road side. If the land is ploughed the seeds get air and water, so they sprout!"

The king was overjoyed at this simple revelation. Isn't it true that we tend to write off our parents and elders by saying, "You don't know anything Dad; times have changed."

Yes, times have changed, but these 'oldies' still know more than we do, because they carry with them the wealth of experience. Knowledge can be acquired through reading, but wisdom is acquired only through practice and experience. It is said that every young man tells his father at some time or the other, "Dad, you are wrong!" But by the time he realizes that his father was right, his own child is old enough to tell him, "Dad, you are wrong!"

3

Who Are You?

"The Guru is the Teacher who removes the fundamental ignorance, which hides the knowledge of this truth from us."

A young man in quest for knowledge came to know of a learned guru. He went up to the cottage of the guru and knocked the door. A stern voice asked, "Who is it?" The young man made an about-turn and came back. The next day he thought of going back to the guru's cottage. As before, he knocked at the door. A voice asked, "Who are you? Where have you come from?"

The boy came back without uttering a word. The following morning, found him knocking the door again. A voice queried, "Who are you? Where have you come from? What do you want?" Sadly the boy retraced his steps and returned.

On the fourth day, this dejected young fellow made his way up the steps of the cottage to find the door open. Without knocking, he went inside. He found a peaceful looking man, sitting cross legged on the floor. He was meditating.

Quietly the boy sat down, a few steps away from him. Sometime later, the guru slowly opened his eyes and his gaze fell on the youngster. He smiled and said, "So you are the one who has been coming here for the last three days. Why didn't you come in?"

The youngster said simply, "You asked me, who I am, where I came from and what I wanted. These are the questions I am trying to find the answers to. I came to you to ask you these questions. I did not have the answers to them, so I went back. Today I found the door open, so I took the liberty of walking in. Can you help me to find the answer to these questions?"

The guru got up and embraced the boy. He said, "Just as a

seeker is in search of a guru, a guru is also in search of the genuine seeker. I am so happy to have you here. It would be a pleasure to teach you!"

Swami says, "The letter *'Gu'* in the word Guru signifies *Gunatheetha* - the one who has transcended the three qualities of Ignorance *(Thamasik)*, Passion *(Rajasik)* and Virtuousness *(Sathvik)* and the letter *'Ru'* signifies the one who is *Roopa Varjitha* (Beyond the Form). The Guru destroys illusion and sheds light; His Presence is ever cool and comforting. He comes to remind people that they have forgotten that they have lost the most precious part within themselves and yet are unaware of it! He is the Physician for curing the illness which brings about the repetitive suffering from birth to death. He is adept at the treatment needed for the cure. If you have not yet got such a Guru, Pray to the Lord Himself to show the way and He will most certainly come to your rescue!"

4

The Best Wife!

"The lentil dish must have just enough salt to make it tasty. Do not spoil the dish by adding too much salt. Similarly, life becomes difficult to bear when you put into it too much 'desire'. Limit your desires to your capacity, and have only those that will grant lasting joy."

It is said that once when Krishna was having a meal with his family, Narada thought of playing a prank to have some fun.

He asked Krishna, "Krishna, you have so many wives; who is your favourite?"

The question raised many eyebrows and put many at unease. It was pretty much known that Rukmini was Krishna's favourite wife, but even Krishna was too embarrassed to spell it out. Rukmini too was worried, about how Krishna would handle this. Krishna looked around and smiled, saying that each of his wives was very dear to him and he loved them all. But Narada, true to his nature, did not give in so easily and prodded further.

So, slowly Krishna looked at all the delectable dishes lying in front of Him and said, "I like all of these. I can't choose a favourite one out of these, so how can I choose a favourite wife?" But Narada, pestered him gleefully.

Then Krishna said, "Jambhvati is like the pure ghee in the food." He described some other wives comparing them to some things on the table and then paused to say "Satya Bhama is like the sweet desert." Krishna mused over the issue carefully avoiding Rukmini's name. But Narada was too smart and asked unashamedly, "What about Rukmini?"

Krishna took a deep breath and said, "Rukmini is like salt." He then got up and everyone dispersed for the day. Rukmini was very upset. All day long, Krishna's words "Rukmini is like salt! Salt! Salt!" kept echoing in her ears.

At dusk when everyone sat down to have their evening meal, there was an uncomfortable silence. Rukmini, sat at the far end, as far from Krishna as she could, her eyes cast downwards.

As the food was served to all, they looked at each other questioningly. Something was wrong with the food... something was missing... the food was bland and tasteless... there was no salt in it!"

Krishna looked at Rukmini, straight in the eyes and smiled, such that her heart turned over in her breast! Everyone knew then! Rukmini! Salt! Oh Lord!

The cook smiled as he realised that Krishna had just put everyone into their places, by one little instruction to the cook... yes, the Lord has His ways.

5

Garbage Food

"Food is God, so don't waste food. If you have excess food, share it with others."

Taruni was a little girl who was the apple of her parents' eyes. Over the years, she had become spoilt, because all her wishes and demands were fulfilled, even before she voiced them completely. All meals were cooked in the house to please her. She would pile up her plate with the delectable dishes that were prepared especially for her. Her little stomach would not be able to take in so much, so the food would go waste. But the parents did not bother to correct her.

One day, as a part of the Value Education Programme, Taruni went on a school trip to a nearby slum. Her teacher and other peers took a walk in the slum and the teacher pointed out to the children, the pathetic living conditions of the slum dwellers. They noticed that a van stopped nearby and dumped two huge black polythene bags and sped away. We as educated people are taught, not to touch unattended objects. But here in the slum, the moment the bags were dropped, all the slum dwellers around, made a dash for them and tore the bags open. Out tumbled bits and pieces of bread, rotis smeared with vegetables, noodles, bits and pieces of salad, silver foil rolled into balls, crumbled paper napkins etc. Everything was just dumped into the bags. It was all a big mess, but for the slum dwellers, it was a treat. They hungrily grabbed whatever they could lay their hands on and stuffed it into their hungry mouths.

Taruni stood, rooted to the spot. She couldn't believe it. Those people were eating food that was practically garbage! The teacher called out, "Come on children, it is time to go ... Taruni, come child it's getting late." But Taruni wasn't listening. The teacher shook her by the shoulder. Then Taruni said, "Ma'am what are these people doing?" The teacher paused for a moment and said, "It seems a nearby restaurant, collects all the leftover food, and drops it off here every day. These people eat it for want of anything better. It may seem inhuman to you but the restaurant owner is actually doing them a favour."

"But Ma'am, how can they eat it? It is garbage!" whispered Taruni in disbelief. The teacher replied in a sombre tone, "Perhaps, they've wasted a lot of food in their last birth, so they have to eat it now!"

We are living in a world where a large number of people do not have enough food to satisfy their hunger. Yet we waste, unmindful of how wrong it is to do so. It is always better to give to those in need than to let good food go down the drain. It is the responsibility of parents to teach their children not to waste food. Needless to say, example is better than precept.

6

Rudrabhishekham

"You say that God knows and sees everywhere, but you also do something wrong with the belief that God is elsewhere at that time."

MILK

On the occasion of *Shiv Rathri*, a huge vessel was placed at the door of the temple for collection of milk. A small notice was placed alongside saying, "Anyone desiring to contribute milk for the *Rudrabhishekham* (Ceremonial bath of the *Shiva lingam*) may pour it into this vessel."

From morning onwards, people started coming in, with their contributions. Each one would lift the lid of the vessel; empty out his pot; put the lid back and leave. During the course of the day, the head priest of the temple thought that he too should pour in at least one pitcher full of milk as his personal contribution to the *Rudrabhishekam*. As he was about to fill up his pitcher with milk, a thought crossed his mind. So many people were pouring milk into the vessel. If he poured in a pitcher full of water instead of milk, who would come to know? The water would mix with the milk and no one would notice anyways! So the head priest filled up a pitcher of water and slyly went up to the designated vessel and putting on a holier than thou face, nattily poured the water into the vessel and covered it again.

A few hours later, it was time for the Rudrabhishekham to begin and the large vessel was brought to the place of the *Pooja* and placed near the *Shiva Lingam*. Amidst chanting of "*Om Namah Shivaya! Om Namah Shivaya! Shivoham! Shivoham!*" the head priest removed the lid from the vessel and filled a small bowl from it to start the *Abhishekham*. But what was that? The bowl didn't have milk in it, it contained water! How could that be so? Everyone had been pouring milk into it since morning! The priest looked around uneasily. The thief in him pricked his conscience. Was this an act of God? Had He turned all the milk into water, to expose the head priest in full public view? As he looked around sheepishly, he realized that guilt and shame was writ large on the faces of all present. Then it dawned on him. Each person had had the same thought. Each one of them had poured water instead of milk, thinking that the others were contributing milk so his act would go unnoticed.

This is the state of the society today. By and large, most people, whatever positions they may be in, are corrupt. Each one thinks of fleecing the system, thinking that no one would know. But eventually the truth does come out. The only person you end up deceiving, is yourself!

You may deceive some people, all the time. And you can deceive all the people, some time. But you cannot deceive all the people, all the time! Most importantly, you cannot deceive God. Remember, each one of us is answerable to the God within us. Each one of us is answerable first of all to our own conscience and later on, to anyone else.

7
Justice by the King

"When the Lord metes out a punishment, it may appear harsh. The penalty depends on the time, place and the circumstances in which the Lord acts."

The Caste System as it was

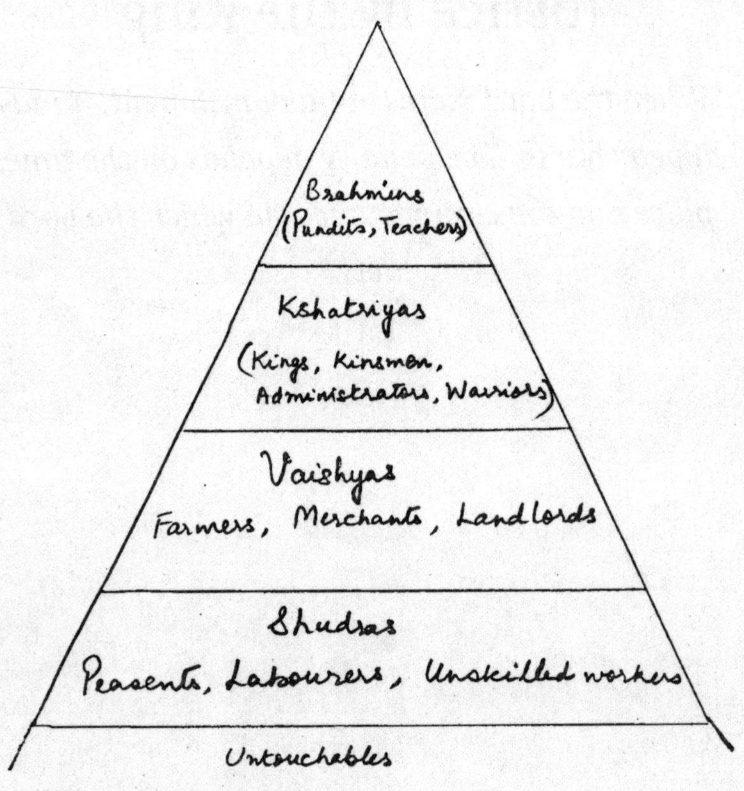

$$4 \times 8 = 32$$

$$4 \times 8 \times 2 = 64$$

$$4 \times 8 \times 2 \times 2 = 128$$

$$4 \times 8 \times 2 \times 2 \times 2 = 256$$

Once upon a time, a matter of theft was brought to the court of a King. The thief was produced before the king and his council of ministers. He had stolen four gold coins from a goldsmith. The fellow begged for forgiveness and promised to return the four gold coins to the rightful owner. Now, this seemed to be enough in the view of the council of ministers, that the property stolen be returned to its rightful owner. But on second thoughts, was it enough? Should not there be a deterrent in the punishment, that the offender does not dare to commit the offence again?

The king here asked the offender, "To which caste do you belong?" The lawyer for the thief asked out of curiosity, "What does that have to do with it? An offender is an offender, whatever may his caste be." But the king had his own viewpoint. He insisted on knowing. The offender turned out to be a Kshatriya. He was fined 128 gold coins!

Why?

The king said, "If you were a Shudra, I would fine you with eight times the value of the stolen goods, so you would have had to pay thirty two coins. Had you been a Vaishya, I would penalise you with twice the amount I would charge from the Shudra, so you would be liable to pay sixteen times. Since you are a Kshatriya, you shall pay double the amount payable by a Vaishya offender. Resultantly, you have to pay thirty two times.Hence, 128 gold coins. And mind you, had you been a Brahmin, I would have charged you double of this too!"

There was a pregnant silence in the court... Why this discrimination? The king went on for the benefit of all present. Responsibilities and privileges he said had to go hand in hand.

The caste of a man is not to be judged merely by his birth. It is to be adjudicated by his education and the profession he follows. Being in a certain position in life he is assumed to be having a certain level of intellect and hence the ability to comprehend the difference between right and wrong as well as the seriousness of the crime. An uneducated person, who is barely able to make ends meet, cannot be expected to be as mentally evolved as an educated person in a responsible position in society. So the punishment should be commensurate with his persona ... physical, intellectual and social too.

The ManuSmriti is said to be the Shastra of Manava Dharma. It says –
"Justice, being violated, destroys;
Justice, being preserved, preserves;
Therefore, justice must not be violated;
Lest violated justice destroy us."

If injustice is done; if a wrong verdict is passed; it is said that the guilt of injustice is borne in four equal parts by the offender, the false witnesses, the judges and the king! Whereas if justice is done, the judges are saved from sin and the guilt falls on the perpetrator alone!

We as Hindus believe in the theory of Karma and past lives. Isn't it true that Justice follows men even after death... even after they leave the body? At many a juncture in life, we wonder at the 'why' of things happening to us or to others around us ... Both good and bad. It makes me think ... perhaps justice is being pronounced!

8
A Hundred Silver Coins!

"The happiness that one derives from virtues is far superior to the happiness that you get from the possession of wealth."

A man had a pouch of silver coins that he had saved over the years. He had finally completed the target figure of a hundred silver coins. One evening his friend was over and he proudly told him that he had collected a hundred silver coins. So passionate was he about the coins that he wanted to show them to his friend. So he emptied out the pouch on the table and carefully started counting them. One, two, three ... twenty eight... seventy four... ninety nine. Where was the hundredth coin? How was this possible, he had counted them just yesterday!

He re-counted them one, two... twelve... twenty four... thirty nine... seventy two... ninety one... ninety nine!

No! It couldn't be! He started all over again for the third time, grouping them into heaps of ten each now. One, two... eighteen... thirty one ... Sixty three... eighty two... ninety two... ninety nine and hundred!!! Yes! Now he got it right! He was happy now! Gleefully he looked across the table to see his friend share his joy. Life was perfect and God was great! It was great to be alive!

A year later, the man was filling ink into his ancient fountain pen. How he loved this pen, which his father had given him on his eighteenth birthday. Old school, but precious nevertheless. The inkpot was almost empty, so he tilted it to one side for the ease of filling up the pen. It slipped and crashed on to the floor and broke! But, wait a moment; what was it that tumbled out of the inkpot? A coin? A silver coin! Oh my God! A silver coin! THE SILVER COIN! Could it be the hundredth silver coin?

His mind flash backed to the day when he had counted his silver coins in the presence of his friend. Twice they had added up to ninety nine. The third time they were a hundred.

Thoughtfully, yet desperately he dialled his friends' phone. "Hey Nimish! Do you remember, you were over at my place for dinner last year in June ... silver coins...ninety nine... hundred... did you put in the hundredth coin?"

He waited with bated breath as Nimish spoke after a taking a deep breath. "Yes my friend, I did!" "But why?" he gasped in amazement. "My friend you were so sure that you had a hundred coins that I thought if you are not able to find the hundredth one, you would think I am a thief. I didn't want to be branded to be a thief so I quietly put a silver coin into your heap."

Sometimes, an honest man has to go to such extremes to keep his character free from blemishes!

9

Together with Trinity

"Someday, one has to give up everything and leave, alone and empty handed. This is the inescapable destiny."

Unusual though it may seem, a man once asked his young son who was a devout follower of Lord Brahma to pray to Lord Brahma for granting immortality to the father. The son replied, "If you wish to become immortal father, I shall surely pray to Lord Brahma for you."

So the young boy performed severe austerities and penance, till Lord Brahma appeared before him and asked him, "My child, I am pleased with your devotion. What is it that you desire?" The boy folded his hands and offered obeisance at the Divine feet of the Lord and replied, "Oh Lord! Your darshan has given me so much happiness that I have no desire for myself. But please grant a boon for my father." "What is it, my dear?" "Please, make my father immortal!"

The Lord smiled and said, "I am the creator. If you want that your father should never meet his end, you shall have to go to Lord Shiva, for He is the destroyer." So the boy and his father accompanied by Lord Brahma, went to Kailash Parvata to seek an audience with Lord Shiva.

Lord Shiva said, "I do perform the act of destruction, but granting immortality is not in my hand, for that you shall have to please Lord Vishnu. He is the one who preserves and protects." So the boy, his father, Lord Brahma and Lord Shiva, all went to see Lord Vishnu, the protector and preserver of life! On the way they met Narada, who went along with them too. Just as they reached and stood together in the dazzling presence of Lord Vishnu, the boy's father collapsed and died. Tears welled in the boy's eyes. He pleaded, "Lord Vishnu, I came to beg you to grant immortality to my father. And he has died in your very Divine presence, even before I got the chance to place my request before you. Why, my Lord? Why did you do this to my father?"

Lord Vishnu said, "Calm down my child." Lord Vishnu signalled for the life record of the dead man to be brought. The last line in it said, "The point in time when the Trinity of Lord Brahma, Lord Vishnu and Lord Shiva, meet in the presence of this man, his son and Narada; shall determine the time of his death!"

Lord Vishnu said, "Son, the congregation of all of us together has resulted in the death of your father. It is the pre-destined moment of his death, which led to the happening of things that made all of you come here. Whatever is destined to happen has to happen. No one can elude death. Go in peace! You have done your best but you cannot change your father's destiny!"

The will of God always prevails. Man can make efforts but the fruits of labour are always in His hands.

During a discourse, Baba said, "An old man was once warned that there was a cobra on the roadside of the path he proposed to walk through. But he said, he had never seen it and so he did not believe it. Unfortunately for him, he did believe in it later, after it bit him. But then, it was too late to benefit from the information that he had heard earlier. Several leaders had to acknowledge that there is destiny that shapes events in lives, irrespective of individual efforts. Know that everyone has to come to the same conclusion, sooner or later – for, there is a limit to the capacity of the individual to control events in the world. Beyond that, there is an Unseen Hand that takes over the wheel of events. One may call it Destiny, another may call it Providence and the third may call it God – the Names do not matter. What matters is your humility, your ability to wonder, and sense of awe at the grandeur and magnificence of Divinity."

10

The Houseflies

"It is only when man is filled with godly thoughts that he will be rid of sorrow. Hence, what should be given up is worldliness. Then alone Aatmaananda (the Bliss of the Spirit) can be got."

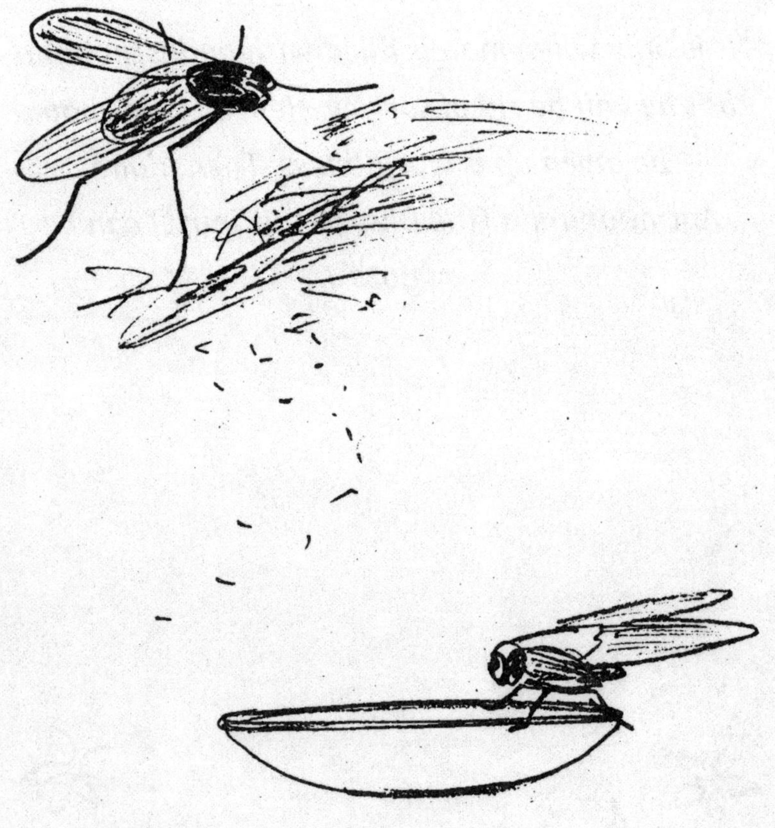

Two houseflies were hovering over a heap of human waste. They would sit on the mound of filth and enjoy the taste of it. Having had their fill, they would start buzzing around from here to there. A little while later, they found a bowl of honey. They sat on the edge of the bowl and slowly ventured on to the shiny golden syrup. Then they tasted it. Oh! It was heavenly! They satisfied their hunger and started flying around again.

Soon they smelt the familiar heap of human feces and landed on it. In this fashion they kept on flitting from the honey to the fecal matter for a long time. They could not decide which one they liked better. While sitting on the honey they would remember the waste and while sitting on the waste they would remember the taste of the honey.

It so happened that a strong gust of wind came. One of the flies was then perched on the honey and its wings got stuck in the honey, so it could not move. It kept enjoying the taste of the honey long enough to forget the taste of the filth and realize that this is what she really wanted. She was in bliss!

The other fly meanwhile was deeply, entrenched in the dirt when the gust of wind came and its wings got smeared with filth, such that it got stuck in the dirt. To make it worse, someone threw some more dirt over the mound and the fly got trapped under it. It struggled while it remembered the honey, but it could hardly breathe now. Sometime later, this fly died.

This is a very ancient story. What does it really signify? We are the fly that flits from the Godly and eternal to the worldly and ephemeral. When we are praying or attending a Religious event, we stay for a while and then rush back to the world. We struggle to spend time in both things but find no peace in either. The gust of wind is the grace of God or the Guru. If He were to hold you and drown you in His love and Grace, you would have no interest left in worldly matters. But you have to seek Him… that is the least you can do!

11

Kaliyuga!

"In this age of Kali, human beings move around like cruel beasts. Compassion is vanishing and ostentation is the order of the day."

We are all aware that we are living in the worst of times in the Kaal Chakra i.e. the wheel of time. This is the period called the Kaliyuga.

Once Krishna was sitting with Arjuna, Bheema, Nakula and Sehdeva. They asked Krishna what life would be like in the Kaliyuga. Krishna looked at each of them and said, "Let me show you, what Kaliyuga will be like." He then shot four arrows from his bow into the four cardinal directions. Smiling, he said, "Now each of you go and get one back."

Arjuna reached the spot where the first one of the arrows had fallen. He picked it up and was about to return when he heard a cuckoo singing an extremely melodious song. Mesmerised by the sweetness in the tone, Arjuna was compelled to go closer. To his utter disgust he saw that the cuckoo was eating the flesh of a dead animal. Arjuna was disgusted and disturbed too. He could not bear to be seeing the gory sight, so he quickly retraced his steps and came back.

Bheema went in search of the second arrow. The arrow had fallen into a dry well. Bheema got the arrow out, but he was intrigued to see that there were four other wells surrounding the dry well. All the four wells were so full that they were brimming with water and water was even flowing out. Confused, Bheema decided not to waste his time on something he failed to comprehend and soon returned back.

The third arrow was traced by Nakula to a spot where a cow had just given birth to a calf. She was licking the calf clean. But as is usually seen, the calf did not stand up after it was clean. The cow kept on licking it, so much so that the calf's skin started to bleed.

The last arrow was found by Sehdev on a mountain full of

boulders. As he picked up the arrow, one of the boulders started to roll downhill. It crushed and hit many trees and rocks, as it rolled down the hill. Eventually it was stopped by a little Tulsi Plant. Sehdev was stupefied at the strange sequence of events.

When all the Pandava brothers, returned to Krishna, they were full of questions. Krishna started to ease their disturbed minds. He said, "In Kaliyuga, the so called caretakers of religion shall have sweet voices and may be well read but they shall misuse their power and positions and shall indulge in all sorts of atrocities like the cuckoo eating the flesh of a dead animal.

In the Kaliyuga, the rich and the poor shall live along side. The rich shall have loads and loads of money. Their coffers shall be overflowing but they shall not offer or share their prosperity with their poor brethren.

Parents shall love their children to such an extent that they shall spoil them with over-indulgence and over protection. The children shall do nothing in their formative years, due to parental love and nothing later due to habit. This overdose of love shall suffocate and destroy these children. The character of people shall deteriorate as fast as the boulder rolling down the mountain. They shall cause injury to many by this descent in character. Eventually *Nama-smarana*, i.e. chanting the name of God shall emerge as the saviour for humanity like the Tulsi plant, as suffering becomes rampant everywhere."

Friends, let not these stories remain to be just stories. Let us learn from our scriptures how to come out of the mess that the world is in. Deep contemplation is required to realise that our lives are given to us for a purpose. The purpose of self-realisation!

12

G. O. D.

"The Lord's ways are mysterious. You do not know the real reasons behind the actions of the Lord."

It was a sunny morning on the beach. A man was sun bathing. He lazed on the warm sand as he watched people doing Para-sailing and jet-skiing a little way off. A young boy was playing a few feet away from where the man lay. He watched the boy collect sand with a little shovel into a bucket and dump it in one place till he made a big mound. He then started shaping it into a castle. The man watched as the boy patted and pushed the sand to carve out the castle walls, doors and windows out of sand. The boy worked tediously for an hour or two. Then he seemed to tire out. He continued but carelessly now, to make the walls and pillars around the castle. He then made a few shabby looking huts by the side.

By the end of it, he was exhausted and lay down on the sand to stretch his limbs. Within a few minutes the boy was up again. He stepped back to admire his work of art. He smiled gleefully as he looked at what was a virtual visual treat.

Then he took another few steps backward and started running towards the castle. All of a sudden he kicked the castle and shattered it completely! The sand got strewn around as it was a few hours before!

The man sat up with a start and almost shouted at the boy as if to ask him, "Why did you do that? You worked so hard to create it?"

But he stopped himself as the truth dawned on him. Isn't this what God is doing all the time? He creates; He enjoys His creation; then He destroys it! That is His play. And this was the child's play!

That's why He is called GOD! G - Generator, O -Operator, D - Destroyer.

The man smiled as he watched the boy pick up his little bucket and shovel and walk away. He thought to himself, "Yes, he is going to create another world somewhere!"

It may not always be easy to comprehend the 'Why?' of everything that God does. He does it for His reasons; for His pleasure! He knows what He wants to make or break and when He fancies doing it. Man is a puppet in His hands. He pulls the strings. Man can only surrender and pray, "Oh God! Use me as you best deem fit, as your instrument. Keep me in the palm of your hand always!"

It also makes me think that He created each one of us with something in mind. He created each one of us with a purpose. Our purpose in life is to find that purpose and live it to the fullest.

13

The Sound of the Pulse

"Have faith that Truth will save you in the long run; stick to it, regardless of what might befall."

An ancient Vaidya (natural healer) had acquired mastery over the science of healing by churning the sacred texts. The length and breadth of India had heard of his superior knowledge and understanding of diseases and their cures. A queen heard of this famous Vaidya and decided to prove him to be not as accomplished as he professed to be. She feigned illness and expressed a desire for this Vaidya to be sent for. The king sent for the Vaidya. It was not considered proper in those times for a woman to be examined by a male physician. So the Vaidya was made to sit on one side of a curtain and the queen was made to sit on the other side. The Vaidya passed a thread to the queen, under the curtain and said, "Your Excellency, please tie this thread around your wrist, so that I can hear the sound of your pulse." He plugged the other end of the string to his ear.

Just in order to prove the Vaidya wrong, the mischievous queen tied the string to the paw of her cat, rather than to her own wrist. The Vaidya on the other side of the curtain heard the beat of the pulse and realized what the queen was up to. He raised his voice and announced loud and clear, "It seems the queen has just eaten a dead rat. It seems she is also about to give birth to kittens!"

The queen was flabbergasted and had no choice but to own up. So instead of exposing the Vaidya, the queen exposed herself! Whatever we do comes back to us in the same way. Life always comes around full circle. Like they say, one who digs a pit for another first falls into it himself!

The news once reported about an Iraqi terrorist Khay Rahnajet, who didn't pay enough postage on a letter bomb that he sent to someone. It came back with 'Return to Sender' stamped on it. Forgetting it was the bomb; he opened it and was blown to bits. Surely what goes around comes around!

14

The Rajasthani Girls!

"All of you are Children of God. So be free from selfishness and manifest the qualities of the Divine Father from today."

I was pleasantly surprised to read an article in The Hindu Newspaper in April 2013 about a village in Rajasthan called Piplantri. Here is the gist of its amazingly inspiring story.

In an era where female foeticide and infanticide is common leading to skewed sex ratios, here is a community that deserves special accolades. It seems, whenever a girl child is born in the village, the villager folk plant 111 trees in her honour in the common areas of the village. The villagers, 8000 in numbers, together care for the saplings to ensure that they grow well. In the last 5-6 years, with an average of 60 girls being born here annually, what a large number of trees have been planted! The trees planted are in the likes of Mango, Neem, Amla, etc. A former Sarpanch (head) of the village who had lost his daughter a few years ago and had started this endeavour in her memory.

At the time the girl is born Rs.10,000/- are collected from her father and Rs.21,000/- are collected from the villagers. A fixed deposit for the entire sum is made in the name of the girl; to mature after 20 years. The parents are made to sign an affidavit that they will send her to school regularly and also look after the trees planted in her name. Also, that they shall not marry her off before the legal age!!!

And here is the best part. The area it seems is termite prone. So, the villagers planted Aloevera plants around the trees in large numbers. Not only the trees, but the Aloevera has also become a source of livelihood for the villagers.

The woman have been trained to harvest the Aloevera to make

juice, gel etc. for which there is a huge market. The village has also banned alcohol and cutting of trees. Crime too has vanished of its own!

This write up in the newspaper touched me immensely. How a small idea can blossom into something so unique and beautiful. The girl child is often considered a liability in India, mainly because of the expense to be incurred at her wedding and even later in life at every small incident; happening or mis-happening. If we can educate our girls and make them as self-sufficient as our boys perhaps people shall stop thinking of girls as a liability.

God made man and woman to complement each other. What a man can do; a woman cannot. Obviously, what a woman can do; a man cannot. What water can do, petroleum cannot and what steel can do, gold cannot. Vice-versa is true too. The mobility of the ant causes it to go about and the immobility of the tree causes it to stay rooted. Every infinitesimal aspect of creation has been designed with a quantum of uniqueness to serve a purpose that can be fulfilled only by being that unique self.

15

Uneasy Lies the Head that wears the Crown

"Be like a trustee, so far as family, riches, reputation, knowledge and skills are concerned. Leave them gladly aside, when the call comes."

Like all kings, this one's head too lay uneasy. There were unending matters of state that needed to be administered, solved, nurtured etc. The king was wise and just. He was hardworking and well respected by his people. But one day he just fell so hapless and tired of being overworked that he wanted to get away from it all.

He went to his Guru and pleaded, "I am tired of this never ending routine of solving people's problems. However many I dispose of, a greater number of problems is ready and demanding my attention, the next day. The tension and enormity of it all is killing me. I want to just lead a simple life, like a commoner.

The Guru said, "So, what is stopping you? Leave the kingdom and go away! "That will make the problem worse! Who will run the empire?" asked the king.

"If you are so concerned about the well-being of the empire, give it to your son, while you live your own kind of life."

"My son is too immature, he wouldn't know how to run it," said the king despairingly.

"Then gift it to me, while you make a life just as you wish to," said the Guru, matter-of-factly.

The king said, "Hmmm. Okay, I think this is a good idea." So the kingdom was formally handed over to the Guru and the king was a free man.

The king got up to take leave; he took a few steps towards the palace. The Guru, stopped him saying, "Where are you going now?"

The king said, "I'm going to the palace to get some money. I will go away to a far off land and start a small business to earn a livelihood." The Guru said, "The Kingdom now belongs to me, you cannot take any money from there."

The king looked thoughtful. Then he said, "In that case, I shall have to look for a job."

The Guru smiled and said, "In case you are looking for a job, I offer you the job of running the kingdom for me. You have the requisite work experience. I won't get a better caretaker than you. What do you say?" The king said, "Okay. I'll take the job." The Guru continued, "Go and run the kingdom on my behalf. Remember that you don't own anything. I shall pay you a salary, but nothing shall belong to you."

So the king went back and began to run the empire as the Guru's caretaker. Some months later the Guru came to the palace and asked the king how he was doing. The king looked very happy. He said, "Now, I am able to solve everybody's problems, without any tension. I worry about nothing, because nothing belongs to me. I just do my job and plan no further. I work hard all day and sleep well all night. I am a very happy man now."

This is what Bhagwan Baba tells us. He says that you are not the doer. Everything is done by Him. He just uses you as His instrument. Nothing belongs to you. Everything is God's. You just get to use it for some time or for a life time. When it is time for you to leave, you have to leave everything behind.

As long as we believe that 'I' am everything, there is no peace. As soon as we dissolve the 'I' into 'Him' everything just falls into place in an instant.

16
Black Coal

"The company of the good and the godly will slowly and surely chasten and cleanse persons prone to stray away from the straight path towards self-realization."

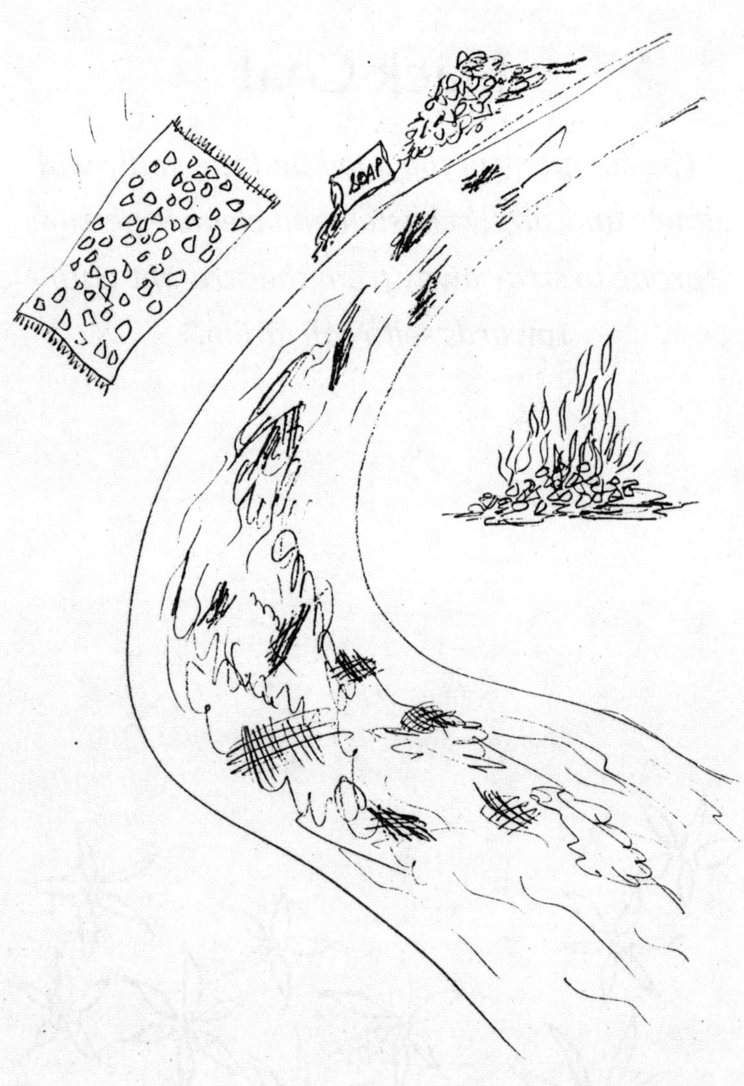
SOAP

The ancients tell of a village headman called Dhanadeya. One day he received an invite from the King to attend a congregation at the Palace. This made him swell up with pride at the sheer honour conferred upon him. He got a new set of clothes made for the occasion. The outfit was fashioned out of pure silk and was white in colour.

So on that day, Dhanadeya donned his white silken finery; completed the effects with golden embroidered shoes and a generous splash of perfume. He preened himself at the mirror and started his journey, ever careful not to let anything stain his spotless white attire. Much as he was careful, but somehow he brushed against a cart carrying black coal and the side of his Kurta got stained with soot. That upset him a lot, but there was nothing he could do about it and the congregation was about to begin.

So Dhanadeya attended the congregation wearing the stained white kurta. During the talks with the King and his courtiers, he forgot the black stain and had a good and fruitful discussion. The meeting got over and he started back home. It was then that he noticed the black stain and his anger flared. He vowed to cleanse all the coals of their blackness so that they couldn't blacken anyone's clothes ever again.

He ordered all the coal in his village to be collected and brought to the bank of the stream that flowed there. Nearly 100 tons of coal was collected and obviously about 50 tons of soap was arranged to wash the blackness off the coal. 10 servants were started on the job, early next morning. The more they scrubbed, the more the blackness flowed out till the stream turned virtually black. Needless to say the black colour could not be washed off the coal.

A wise man passing by, saw the whole drama and offered to help cleanse the coal and make it white. Dhanadeya, who was at his wit's end, by the washing activity, agreed to take help from the wise man.

The man quickly spread out all the coal on the ground and let it dry. After the coal dried up, the man set the coal on fire. It burned all night. The next morning white ash was left behind! Dhanadeya understood that it was only fire that could do the job of getting the coal rid of its black colour. Water couldn't do it.

In this world we are like coals. We need to burn our desires and vices to connect with God, and get the dirt off our souls. No amount of worldly pleasure can give the bliss that the experience of Namasmarana or connecting with God can give!

17
Kalpataru

"You are the creator of your own destiny. Be self-confident; that is, have confidence in yourself. For, that self is Divine."

Ancient Indian mythology tells of Kalpatarus. These were wish fulfilling trees that could grant a person anything that he wished for the moment he wished for it. The word 'Kalpana' means wish and 'taru' means tree. So a tree that could grant or fulfil wishes was called Kalpataru.

The young traveller was crossing through a lonely jungle. Being tired, he lay down under a tree to rest, not knowing that the tree where he lay was a Kalpataru. He was hungry and said, "How I wish I could get some food. I'm so hungry." Before he could finish saying this, a plate, well-laden with steaming hot food appeared before him. As he got up to eat the food, he thought, if only there was someone to fan me in this heat; a beautiful girl perhaps! Out of nowhere a beautiful damsel appeared, holding a decorative cloth fan and started fanning him. He smiled happily and said, "Oh! I wish I could marry you, Oh beautiful lady!" At that moment, garlands of flowers appeared in their hands. They exchanged garlands and performed a "Gandharva Vivaha!"

The man said, "I wish to have many children." Just then there were many young boys and girls around them addressing the couple as "Mother!" "Father!" By now the man started getting a little intimidated. He said, "Oh! My God! So many children! When they grow up they will fight amongst themselves ..."

The man shrieked in agony, "Don't fight my children. If you do so, I will die ..."

Just as the words 'I will die' escaped his lips, the traveller died. The woman with the fan and the children ... all vanished.

Heaven or hell they say is created in our own minds. Whatever we think, is what happens. A spider weaves a web and then gets caught in it, isn't it?

A person can change his world by changing his thoughts. There are people who revel in self-pity. But who is to blame? Each person is responsible for his own destiny to a large extent. Look into the mirror. What do you see?

If you smile, you get a smile in return.
If you frown, you get a frown in return.

The world around you is a mirror image of the chaos or beauty inside you.

Everything is created twice in this world. Once in the mind of the creator and thereafter on a physical plane! So think only good and positive thoughts, so that even if you get entangled in your own web, at least it will be a happy one!

You have the power to draw your own world. You have the power to paint it in the colours you want to. It is in your hands. And the onus for making it lies only with you. At the same time, if what you have created is not a pleasant picture, you have nobody to blame except yourself! So take charge of your life. Pick up your paint brush and go bindass! Follow your heart and soul; you can't go wrong!

18

Change Your Destiny!

"If one rises above the body to the level of the heart, then the divine qualities of prema (love), daya (compassion), sahana (patience), and sahanubhuti (empathy) all manifest in the person."

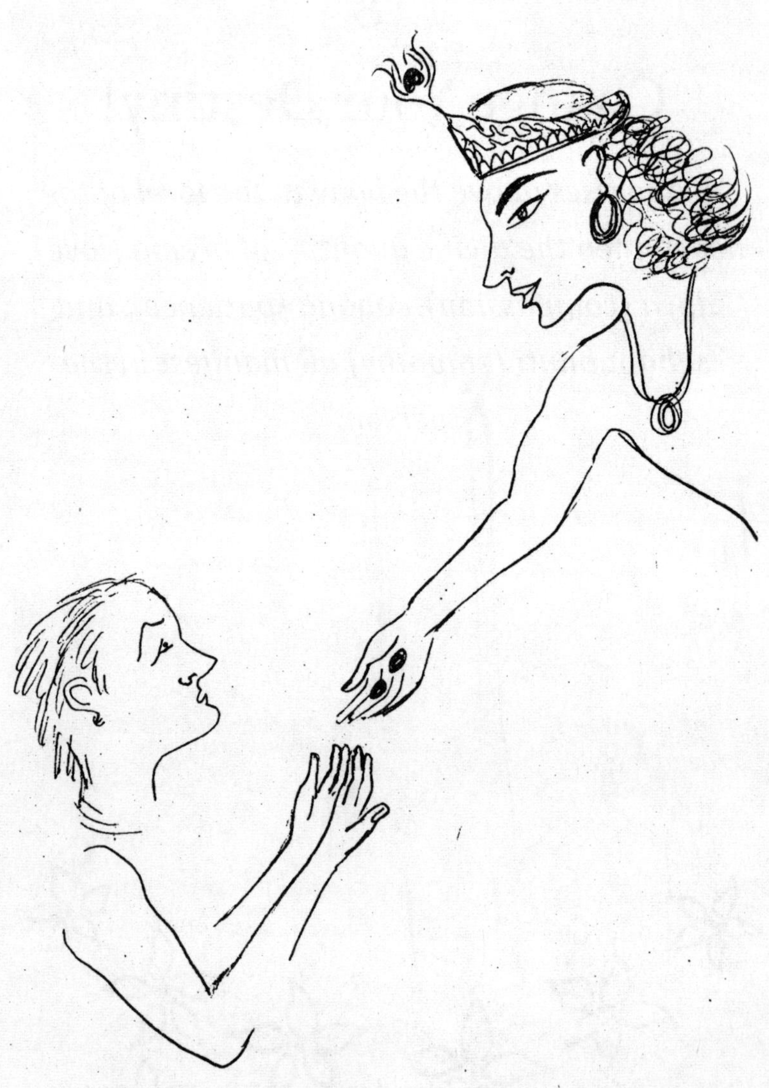

Krishna and Arjuna were taking a stroll when they came across a Brahmin who was begging. Arjuna out of pity gave him a pouchfull of gold coins. The Brahmin was overjoyed and set off for home with a romantic song in his heart and dreamy eyes. On the way, a robber looted him.

So, on the following day, he was out begging again. Arjuna was surprised to see him. On hearing his story, Arjuna felt pity again and gave him a valuable gem and made sure that the man hid it in his pocket while going home. The Brahmin hid it in an old mudpot that was lying unused for a long time in his house. His wife had gone out to fetch water from the river. On her way back she fell down and her pot of water broke. So she went home and quietly picked up the old mud pot and went to fetch water. The Brahmin was fast asleep. The moment she lowered the pot into the river to fill it, the gem fell out. She went home totally unaware of the loss that she had just caused.

The Brahmin cursed his destiny when he realised what had happened. The next day, he was back to begging again. Isn't it true that we may give something, to another, but we cannot change another's destiny?

But, God can! Read on ...
When Krishna and Arjuna heard the tearful story of the poor Brahmin, Krishna quietly gave two paisa to the Brahmin. Arjuna exclaimed, "Oh Deenbandhu! I could not redeem him of his poverty even by giving him so many gold coins and the precious gem. What difference will two paisa make? Perhaps it is his destiny, that he shall always be a beggar!

Krishna just smiled. The Brahmin too was baffled with the

paltriness of Krishna's donation, especially in contrast with Arjuna's largesse.

On the way home he saw that a fisherman had just caught a fish, who was gasping for life. He felt pity for the poor creature and thought to himself, "These two paisa, will not be enough to buy me even a meal. So, let me buy the fish and save its life." So the Brahmin bought the fish for two paisa and immediately put it into his begging bowl and poured water into it. He set off towards the river to release the fish. He then noticed that the fish spat out something. It was the same precious gem that Arjuna had given him that he had hid in the mud pot!

The Brahmin was overjoyed. In his ecstasy he exclaimed, "I found it, I found it..." Coincidentally the robber who had looted him of his pouch full of gold coins were sitting just there. He thought the Brahmin had recognised him and was shouting, "I found him, I found him ..." Fearing that he would be taken to the king's court and punished, he begged the Brahmin to pardon him and also returned the gold coins.

Arjuna was astounded! He said, "Krishna, what I could not achieve by giving so much, you have achieved by giving so little! What is this mystery?"

Krishna smiled his beautiful, bewitching smile and said, "Both times when you gave to him, he thought only of his personal comforts and the betterment of his life. When I gave him, he thought about the woes of another living creature. Truly speaking, when someone shows sympathy and helps someone, he is doing my work. When he is doing my work, how can I not do his?"

19

Give Up Anger!

"Train your mind to walk quietly along small stretches of road at first and then after you have become sure of its docility, you can take it along safely down the tortuous road of the six fold temptations of lust, anger, greed, delusion, pride and jealousy."

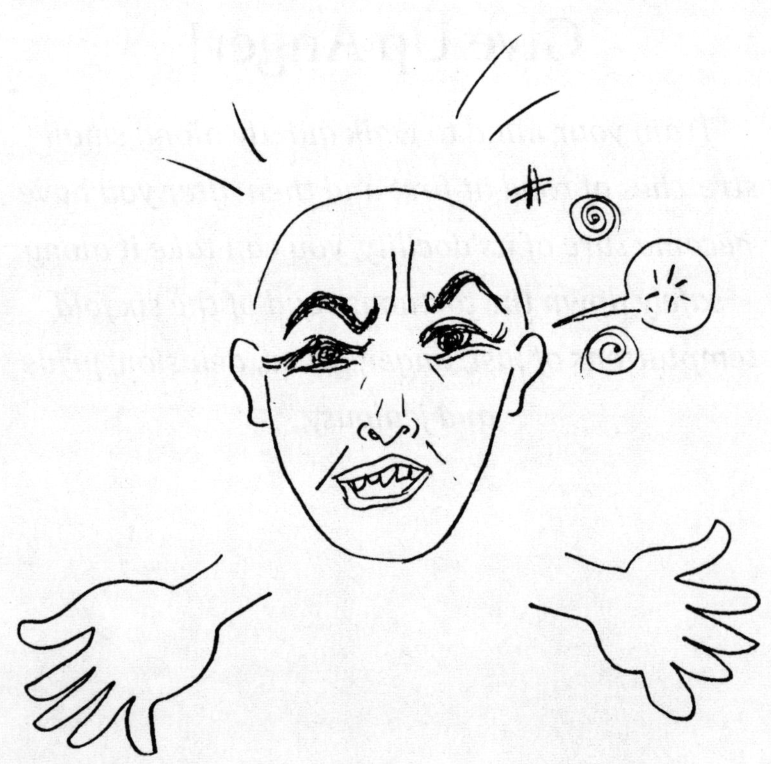

A preacher was also the head of a village and had a large number of people at his beck and call.

As part of his discourse on the holy day of Dusshera, he talked about the vices of Ravana and the importance of giving up vices and bad habits. So he encouraged and goaded everyone to give up one bad habit each on this auspicious day. To set an example, he said, "I give up my anger. From now on, I will never get angry."

As the discourse concluded and the congregation started to disperse, a little girl came up to the preacher and said, "Oh Guruji, which bad habit did you give up!" He said, "I gave up my anger!"

Another youngster asked, "Did you really give up your anger?" The priest raised his head pompously and said, "Of course I did! I shall never be angry again!" As he walked a few steps ahead, a man said, "Guruji, what a wonderful resolve, but do you really think, you will be able to carry it off?" The Guru said, "Do you think, I will go back on my word? Of course I will do it!"

A few minutes later a girl asked, "Guruji! Did I hear you right? What did you gave up?" He asked, "Oh Lord! I am telling you all, I have given up my anger!" Another minute later an old lady said, "I was sitting too far behind, so I didn't really hear you. What did you say, you gave up?"

Now, that was getting to be too much! The preacher shouted, "How many times should I tell you? I have given up my anger!"

Well! Giving up vices or working on self-improvement is not such a simple matter. It takes huge mental strength and resolve. It is not as simple as making an announcement of renunciation. Character and countenance cannot be built in a day. It is a never ending process in self grooming. We can never achieve much if we are in a hurry to achieve. One learns to walk first and later on to run. When one foot walks, the other rests ... howsoever fleetingly it may be! Doing and being are to be balanced at all times!

20

The Crow's Feathers!

"You should teach students discipline, humility and respect, and instill in them the spirit of service and the sense of fellowship. Imbue your children with confidence and courage. Unify them through love and love alone; give no room for anger, jealousy or hatred within you and teach the children the three P's: Purity, Patience and Perseverance. Armed with these three qualities, your students can protect the nation better than any army or atom bombs."

In the school parking lot was a large Peepal tree. There was a crow's nest on it. The boys were to park their bicycles in the parking lot. Crow's feathers were often seen strewn around. When the boys entered the final class of high school, their English teacher made a strange request. "Boys, this is your final year in school. I am a collector of crow's feathers. If ever you see one fallen in the school, do pick it up and give it to me."

So, all through the year, someone or the other would find a crow's feather and give it to the teacher. On the last day of school was a farewell dinner organized for the outgoing class. Each of the boys was asked to come up to the dais and collect his certificates. The Principal handed over the certificates to each boy with a pat on the back and a word of encouragement to some; and a rap on the back with a word of reprimand to others. The English teacher handed over to each boy, a feather!

The feathers had all been painted golden or silver. Each of them had a message written on it. The messages were like:

1 There is no substitute for hard work. Never give up!
2 Whenever in doubt, look up and you shall find God smiling down at you!
3 You are special. Add value to the world!
4 You are the brightest star in the sky!
5 Surf the inner net before you surf the internet!

Thirty years down the line, Amitas a CEO at a BPO was in deep thought. Business was going down. Costs were on the incline and receipts were on the decline. Attrition rate in the staff was unusually high. To put it concisely, things were just not good. In an endeavor to find some peace, Amitas had taken a weekend holiday trip to a resort in the hills at Shimla. He sat in the sun, a medley of thoughts zig zagging through his tired brain. His ten year old daughter cut through his thoughts, “Papa, I want to have corn on the cob. Let's go to the market place.” Absent mindedly he reached for his wallet to give her some money saying, “Honey, why don't you and your brother take a stroll and get it. I just want to be lazy.” As he opened his wallet, a golden feather fell out of it. His daughter asked, “Papa, what's that?”

He looked at it thoughtfully and said, “A teacher from school gave it to me. But I haven't looked at it for ages.” She peered closely and read the half faded words inscribed on it, “Whenever in doubt, look up and you shall find God smiling down at you.”

Spontaneously, the father and daughter raised their heads to look up. Up above, on the balcony of the second floor, stood an old man. He waved and smiled at them. A shiver ran down Amitas's spine. Hurriedly he ran upto the balcony. “Excuse me, aren't you Raghavendra Sir.”
“Yes, I am,” slowly said the old man.
“Sir, I am Amitas, I was your student in school. You gave me this feather.”

For what seemed like eternity, the two men chatted and caught up on the thirty years that had elapsed. Strangely, the heart to heart talk seemed to ease out the tensions in his mind. Surely coincidences are incidents where God chooses to remain silent, but He is surely looking on!

At the next annual school reunion, Amitas made it a point to invite Raghavendra Sir, as the Guest of honour. And guess what? Most of the boys recounted having treasured their feathers. Emotional stories tumbled out and bonded the boys even closer. Here were birds of a feather, flocking together and you know who was smiling with tear filled eyes, don't you?

21
Fable of Kidas

"If you want to experience the Divine, you must give up pomp and pride."

There is a fable of a learned man who was recognised for his intelligence and appointed minister to the king. One hot summer day he was out in the forest and became very very thirsty.

He saw a dilapidated hut and a well nearby. A little girl was drawing out water from it. He said, "I am thirsty. Give me some water, little girl."

She said - I will give it to you, but I don't know you, so first you must introduce yourself.

Kidas - I am a very great person. You are a child so you don't know me. If the elders in your house were to see me, they would recognise me.

Girl-No, no! There are only two great personalities in the world and I know them well. You are not one of them... Do you know who they are?

Kidas -I am scorched by the heat and I don't know who they are. I only know that I am thirsty. Please give me some water or I will faint.

Girl-See! How can you be great if you are going to faint just out of such a trivial thing as thirst? The only great ones are Food and Water. Without them, see what has happened to you! Now tell me who you are...

Kidas -Okay, so I am an eternal traveller. Now, can I have some water?

Girl-How can you be an eternal traveller? You are already exhausted! There are only two of those and I know them well.

Do you?

Kidas -No, I don't. Why are you irritating me? I am asking you to give me some water.

Girl-I will if only you tell me the names of those two.

Kidas- I don't know. You tell me who they are.

Girl-They are the Sun and the Moon. They have been travelling since the beginning of time and continue to do so untiringly.

So saying the girl entered her hut and disappeared from sight. Kidas was at his wits end. He knocked at the door. An old woman came out with a pot and headed straight for the well. She too proceeded to draw out clear and pure water from it.

Kidas had lost some of his pompousness by now. Very politely he said - Amma, please give me some water. I am thirsty.

Woman-I don't know you. Who are you?

Kidas- I am a guest.

Woman- There are only two guests in the world. They are Money and Youth. They come for a short period. How can you be a guest?

Kidas-Alright if I am not a guest, I am one who has patience. I have been patiently asking for water. But I can hold on no longer now. Have mercy, or I shall die.

Woman-No! There are only two in this world who are patient.

They are the Earth and the trees. Man uses and abuses them but they patiently and silently keep giving more and more. You are not patient by any standards.

Kidas-Oh Lord! Then I am stubborn. I shall not give up till you give me some water.

Woman-There are only two who are stubborn. They are the nails and the hair. Howsoever much you cut them, they grow again.

Kidasb -What should I do to please you? Alright I am a fool. Now, will you give me some water?

Woman-Ha ha! There are only two fools. They are the king who rules without being fit for the throne and the King's Chief Advisor who proves wrong things right, just to please the king.

Kidas was speechless. He felt at the feet of the old woman.

Kidas-Mother, please don't test me further. Have mercy on me!

Just then there was a heavenly voice, saying, "Rise up Kidas, your pride and ego had swelled up beyond limits, so I had to enact this drama to bring you to your senses."

As he raised his head, he saw the old woman smile as she lovingly poured water into his out stretched palms and quenched his thirst.

Our youngest son Satyam, has written more than 400 poems sitting in Sai Kulwant Hall, inspired by the beauty of Swami and His world. Here is one of them that he wrote looking at the beautiful flower decorations one festive evening in the Mandir...

There is only one Religion, the Religion of Love

To unify all flowers of the world,
To teach all of them to stay together,
To preach that their unity was the key,
To a peaceful and enlightened world.

I saw many concentric circles of flowers,
The innermost and the outermost being red.
Enveloping all the other garlands,
That were yellow, orange and white.

And the Lord told me that they began and ended
At the same red emotion of love.
That love was what, that beautified and illumined.
All the other religions inside it.

For love was the beginning and end of every religion,
As Swami's voice beckoned,
There is only one religion, the religion of love.

Satyam Tandon

22

The Passport Officer!

"You will be blissful the moment you give up ego and attachment."

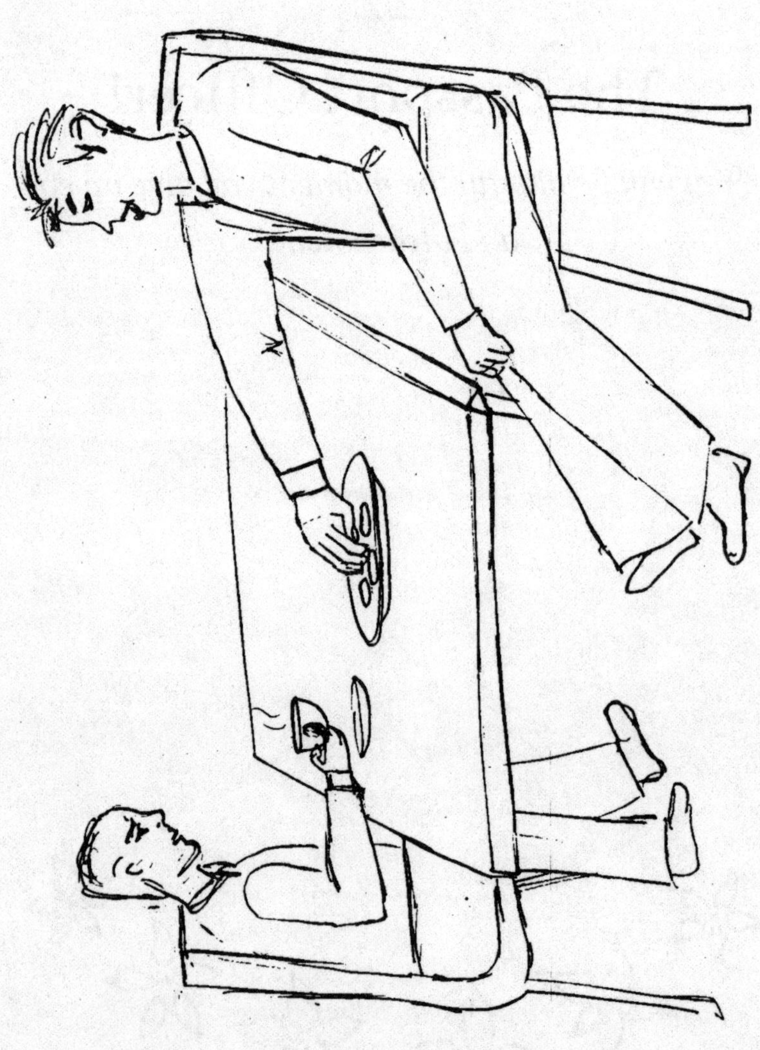

In a queue outside the passport office, a man and his friend reached the client window, and the passport officer said brusquely, "Time up. Come tomorrow." The man's friend, called out, "Hey! Hello! My friend ..." The man said, "Forget it, he will not listen, did you not see the look of contemptuous finality on his face?"

The friend said, "This is shameful ... anyways you wait under the tree there. Let me try." The friend found the passport officer having a cup of tea in the cafeteria and sat on the chair opposite him. The Passport Officer raised his eyebrows questioningly. The friend smiled. The Passport Officer was unnerved, "What do you want?" he mumbled. "Nothing, I just came in for a cup of tea. I found you sitting alone, so I thought I could sit with you." "Hmm, that's because nobody likes me here. So I always sit alone," he said tersely. He picked up a biscuit from the officer's plate. "Have you ever thought why no-one likes you here?"

"It doesn't matter. Anyways no one likes me anywhere. My life is such. My wife left me and she even took my children with her." "So, did you try to find out why she left you?" The officer looked at him, sometimes with uncertainty and sometimes with hatred, as the friend continued to munch on his biscuits.

Finally the friend said, "Look around, everyone in the cafeteria is sitting with someone or the other. Look at yourself, why are you left alone? Let me tell you. You snap at everyone who crosses your path. You are ready to bite and bark at anyone who comes close to you. A few minutes back, you banged the window shut in the face of the last man in the queue. Did you see his face? He had been standing in the queue for five hours. It would have taken you just another five minutes. And you told him to come tomorrow! Can you imagine how he would have felt? My friend, life is not just about making money. It's about making friends too. I too came here only to help a friend."

The officer rolled up his eyeballs and said, "Too late now. The fellow would have gone away." "No, he is sitting under the tree outside. Should I call him? Will you stamp his papers?" With much difficulty, the Passport officer swallowed his pride and said, "Yes."

Ten years later. The friend got a call from a man who said, "Sir, I am the Passport Officer ..."

The story told by him was such ... Read on ...
With each passing day the passport officer became softer and kinder to his colleagues and started making friends out of foes. One day, he visited his wife. She was having lunch. He went and sat on the chair next to her and said, "How are you?" She said nothing. He picked up a piece of roti from her plate and put it into his mouth. He said, "I'm hungry too." With tears in her eyes she pushed the plate towards him and said, "You eat this. I'm not really hungry." So, together the estranged couple shared a meal and bridged the gap of a number of years, cementing it with tears of joy and sorrow. To cut the long story short, the wife returned to live with her husband and so did the children. Now, his daughter was grown and he was calling to invite the friend to come and bless her at her wedding. And he said, "Sir, now I don't just make money, I make a lot of friends too!"

How beautiful are the ways of God. Sometimes, He sends His message through someone in such a crisp way. But we don't take the message, because it is not packaged in the way we want it. Almost everyone loves their own... spread your arms, you will be surprised how many you can gather into your embrace!

23

A Few Bricks!

"Today we find many individuals who exploit others for their own happiness. We rarely come across an individual who sacrifices himself for the sake of others welfare."

In the Epic of Mahabharata is cited an incident where Krishna was crossing through a forest along with some villagers. Bhima accompanied them. They sat to rest on the outskirts of a village. A poor old man was walking by. Some boys playing nearby, threw their ball at him. He stumbled and fell. His stick fell to one side and his turban to the other. He cried out in pain, but the mischief mongers laughed at his plight. Bhima went forward and helped the old man get up and restored his stick and turban to him. Feeling very disturbed Bhima asked Krishna, "Can't God see the plight of this old man? Why does He make people suffer? Why doesn't He punish those insolent boys?"

Krishna hinted a smile and ignored the questions. He looked around and said, "Bhima, everyone is hungry. We should cook some food. Will you get some bricks so that we can make a fireplace to cook something? Meanwhile the others can gather up some firewood." So Bhima went towards the village to look for bricks. He looked around for some time, but could not find any loose bricks or even stones. He saw a beautiful well-built house. Behind it he saw a dilapidated house that was pretty much in ruins. In his search for bricks, he punched the wall of the run down old house and few bricks fell apart. He picked up a few and returned to his people. They made a fireplace and cooked some dinner. As they were eating, Krishna casually asked Bhima, "Brother Bhima, wherefrom did you get the bricks?" So Bhima told Him that he had searched in vain till he found an old and run down house behind a mansion, so he punched a hole in the wall and got the bricks.

"Hmmm" said Krishna. "A poor man's house obviously ... So why didn't you break the mansion's wall? Bhima retorted, "Why would I break a beautiful mansion, just to get a couple of bricks, when I could have gotten them from a broken down structure anyways?" Krishna smiled mysteriously. All of a sudden Bhima's jaw dropped. Hadn't he done just what the boys had done to the poor octogenarian?

Krishna continued, "So it is my friend. The world is like that. Might is right. The lion feeds on the goat. The cat feeds on mice. The frog feeds on flies. The strong always vanquish the weak. If the weak have to stay alive, they have to strengthen themselves. Opportunities come to all; some take them, some don't!

24
Justice by the Shepherd

"Investigate and examine, then you have the right to pronounce judgement."

King Bhoja was considered to be a just and fair king. One day a Brahmin came to him and said, "I have been away to Kashi on a pilgrimage. Before leaving I gave three precious stones to my neighbor for safekeeping. My wife and small child were at home. Now that I have returned and am asking him for the stones he says that in my absence, he returned them to my wife. My wife says that he did not return them to her. I want justice."

The King asked the neighbour, "Did you return the precious stones entrusted by this man to you." "Yes, your highness, I returned them to his wife." "Do you have a witness?" asked the king.

"Yes, the village headman and the caretaker were there, when I did so."
So the King called the two witnesses and asked them, "Did this man return three precious stones to the Brahmin's wife in your presence?" Both of them confirmed that the stones were returned in their presence.

The King was very angry with the Brahmin for having wasted his time. He accused him of greed and dishonesty and sent him off.

Now, there was a Shepherd boy who sat on a hillock. He was reputed to give very good justice. So the aggrieved Brahmin sought his help. He told the entire story to the shepherd boy.

The boy called the neighbour, the village head man, caretaker and the Brahmin's wife. King Bhoja had also heard of the shepherd boy, so he too decided to go and watch the Shepherd boy decide the case.

The shepherd took the Brahmin's wife aside and softly asked her if she had received the stones. She said, "No."

The shepherd boy then asked the neighbour who maintained his earlier stance saying, "I have returned the stones to the Brahmin's wife."

He then took the village headman aside and asked, "What kind of stones, did the man return to the Brahmin?" The headman replied, "They were as blue as the sea and shone brightly as the moon. They were as big as my fist."

The shepherd then took the caretaker aside and asked the same question. The caretaker said, "The stones were as red as blood and transparent and as big as berries."

The boy then called them all together and said, "The neighbor is a liar. He has deliberately asked these two witnesses to say that he returned the precious stones. He has to return them to the Brahmin."

King Bhoja who had been watching the entire proceedings was impressed.

It is never possible to decide who is right or wrong unless you hear out both sides and understand the problem. Just a cursory glance at any situation may lead to a wrong judgement. Baba says, "You may talk in a flamboyant high-sounding style. Know that you are judged not by your tongue, but by your activity and attitude."

25

The Holy Shadow!

"The company of the holy will inspire him to travel in hope and faith. The assurance that God is within call, that He is ever near, will lend strength to his limbs and courage to his eye."

There was a Saint who performed penance to have Divya darshan. After long and rigorous hours of prayer and meditation, God was pleased and appeared before him. God said, "I am pleased my child. Tell me, what do you want?"

The saint took offence to this question and said, "I prayed out of pure love and devotion ... because I wanted to see you. I don't want anything. I didn't ask for anything. How can you think that I am so selfish?"

God was a little surprised. Now, that was certainly not, run of the mill. Everyone seemed to want something or the other. And God's darshan is not supposed to go in vain. So something ... something had to be given. At the cost of repetition, God asked the saint again, "I am happy, that you asked for nothing. But I still want to give you something. Tell me and I shall grant it to you!" The saint felt downright insulted. He said, "God! I told you I don't want anything.How can you doubt me? I have got your darshan. I am wondering if you are a real God or not ... can't you understand that I desire nothing else?"

So, God smiled and thought to Himself, "This is a unique character. He thinks I am not a real God, because I want to give him something. But anyways, I surely have to bless him with something." So the Lord silently blessed the saint's shadow, saying that wherever his shadow fell, there would be peace, happiness, prosperity and unity... And so it was!

This leads me to think ... There are many saints that move around in society. I don't know how deep a relationship they share with God ... but undoubtedly, meeting a saint does give peace and happiness, even if momentarily - *'Sant-darshan'* is always calming and inspiring. Wherever pure souls go, they spread happiness and peace ... perhaps because their shadows have been blessed by the Lord Himself!!!

26

Nandu's Tea Stall

"People are bereft of gratitude, which is not right. One should be grateful for the help they have received from others as long as one is alive."

Tea
Green Tea
Gold Leaf
Tea
Tea
Tea
Tea
Tea
Tea
Tea
Tea
Tea
Tea
NANDU's TEA STALL

A beggar sat by the curb, holding out a shabby tin container, with a few coins in it. It was a cold day and the wind beat mercilessly through the trees in the foothills in this sleepy town. The beggar pulled his shoddy blanket closer to keep himself warm. Shikhavat Singh, a rich man who owned most of the tea plantations in the vicinity was taking a walk, wearing a smart tweed coat and flannel pants. He wore a warm golf cap and held a handsome walking stick that added class to his purposeful gait. Walking past the Green valley, he noticed the beggar shivering in the cold. He stopped there and asked him, "My friend, why are you begging?" The beggar, though young, looked weary and sick. He said, "Sir, I came to this town looking for work. I have not been able to find a job. I finished all the money I had. I have not eaten a morsel for the last three days. I am begging because I am so hungry and I don't have the strength to go around in search of work anymore." There was a note of honesty in the beggar's voice. So Shikhawat Singh said to him, "How about you and I start a business? What's your name?" The beggar said, "Nandu" as he looked up in disbelief. "Why would you want to start a business with me? I have nothing to contribute, let alone invest." Shikhawat Singh shook his head, smiled and said, "Oh yes! You do! You have a sound mind in a sound body. A few days of good food shall get you back on your feet. Listen, I shall give you a hundred boxes of tea leaves every morning. All you have to do is, set up a little stall on the roadside. This place is swarming with tourists. Just sell the tea leaves and we shall share the profits." Nandu couldn't believe his ears. This was unbelievable. He said, "Sir, what share shall I get, of the profits? 5% ... or?" The gentleman straightened up, adjusted his cap and said, "Oh! We'll work it out. Here take this fifty rupees and have some dinner. Come to me tomorrow morning, at the green bungalow at the top of the hill." So, Nandu became a tea vendor. He worked hard from morning to night. By the end of the month, he had made a handsome profit. So he put it in front of Shikhawat Singh and said, "Sir, this is all due to your benevolence. Give me a small share, as you deem fit." The rich man smiled and picked up half of the money saying, "50% is yours. Keep up the good work." Nandu was beside himself with joy. This was unbelievable. 50% of the profit! Oh Lord! You are great! So the next month came and went and so did the following one. Nandu was in good health and spirits. The colour had returned to his cheeks and his eyes shone bright and happy. Another few months later, when Nandu came to Shikhawat Singh to handover his share of profit, he had a disgruntled look on his face. He thought to himself, "Why do I have to give half of the profit to this rich guy? After all, I do all the hard work. What does he do?" So in the following months, he paid the profit but most unhappily. A day came when he said the unpleasant words that had been bottled up in him, to Shikhawat Singh. Shikhawat Singh smiled as he always did and said, "My friend, all the share of profit that you had given to me, lies safely with me. It is yours. I have saved it for you. In future you can decide if you want to share the profits with me or not." This is life. God gives us opportunities to work and earn. Initially we promise to pay back a share of the grace. Sometime later, we don't want to do it, because we become greedy. Money should not be allowed to go to the head; it should remain confined to the pockets. Just like a boat sailing in the water is a good thing, but if the water gets into the boat; it becomes the cause for it to drown.

27

A Thousand Years or a Moment

"The mind must become bhakthimaya (saturated with devotion to God). The intelligence must be transformed into Jnana (divine knowledge)."

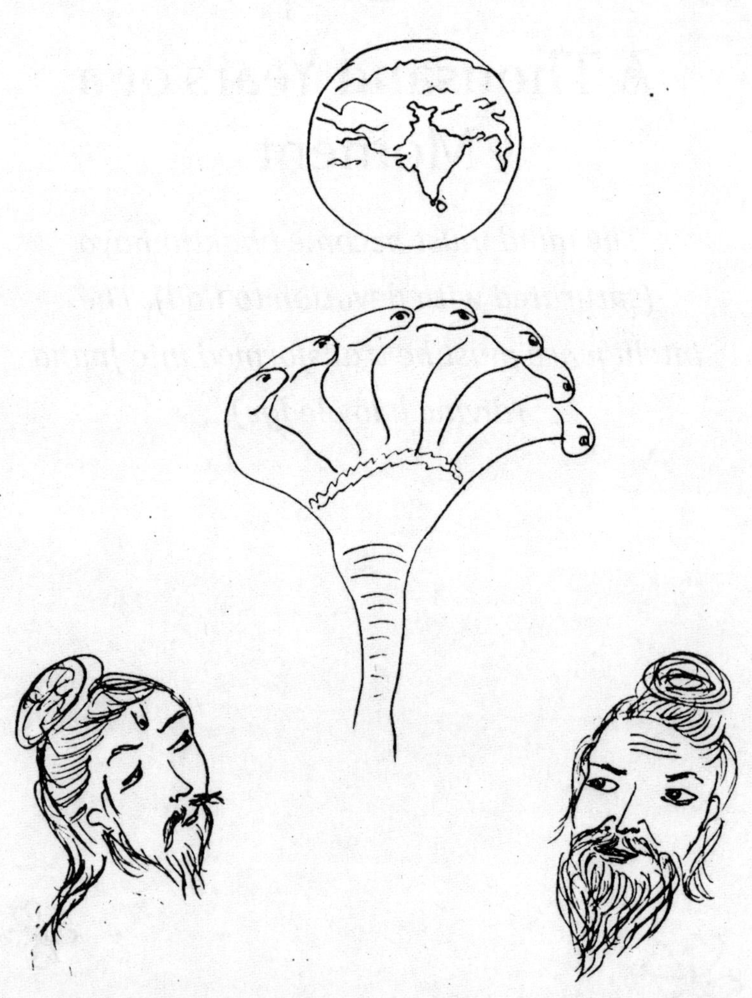

The Epic Ramayana has innumerable little anecdotes in it that hold a lot of meaning. Here is one of them.

It is said that once Sage Vashistha visited the hermitage of Sage Vishvamitra who gifted the fruit of one thousand years penance to Sage Vashistha. Sometime later, Sage Vishvamitra, visited Sage Vashistha, who gifted him the fruit of one moment of Satsangh. Satsangh is Satya-sangh i.e. in the company of truth. Time spent in the company of the devotees of God, listening to or singing the praises of God or His devotees is commonly called satsangh. Sage Vishvamitra felt very insulted and thought, "Does he consider that one moment of his satsangh is equal to my one thousand years of penance?" Sage Vashistha understood what the former was thinking by the looks on his face. He said, "Vishvamitra, it seems you have some doubt about the value of Satsangh. Let us go to a learned person and ask for help to settle the issue."

Together they went to Lord Brahma, who said, "I am busy all day long with the cause of creation. Where do I have the time to think of such things? It is better if you ask Vishnu." So they went to Lord Vishnu. He said, "This is a question that can be answered by one who does a lot of penance and meditation. Perhaps you should ask Shiva."

The duo proceeded to Mount Kailash. Lord Shiva was just about to start his meditation session, so He said, "I would be late for my meditation if I engage in trying to solve the issue. I think you should best go to Sheshanaga and seek his help." So saying, Shiva closed His eyes and started to meditate.

The two sages went to Sheshanaga, who as per legend holds the Earth up on its head. They posed their problem to the Shesha. He said, "Well Sage Vishvamitra, you see I balance the Earth on my head all the time, so with so much weight on my head, I really cannot think. Would you hold the Earth up for a few seconds, so that I can apply my mind to the problem?" Sage Vishvamitra replied, "How can I do that Shesha? I am not so strong!" "The serpent replied, "So use the strength of one thousand years of penance and request the Earth to lift itself up for a second from my head." Immediately Sage Vishvamitra took a handful of water and said, "Oh Mother Earth! I give you the fruit of one thousand years of penance. Please raise yourself above Sheshanaga's head for a few seconds, so that he can think." That being said, but the Earth did not budge!

Then the Sheshanaga told Sage Vashishtha, "Now you gift one moment of Satsangh to the Earth and request her." Sage Vashishtha took a handful of water and said, "Oh Mother Earth! I gift you the fruit of one moment of Satsangh. Please raise yourself from the head of the Sheshanaga, just for a few seconds."

Immediately the Earth raised itself and the Sheshanaga's head was free from the load! Then Vishvamitra eagerly said, "Now your head is free, now think and tell us quickly, which one is more potent?"

The serpent smiled, a thousand headed smile and said, "Do you still need an answer?"

28

Celestial Dancers!

"God alone is your anchor, who will save you from stress and storm."

Indian Mythology is so rich and there is so much to learn from the little anecdotes therein. Every time I read a mythological text, I find a treasure. Here is one of them.

Indra, the King of the Devas had a thousand wives. One day his wife Indrani asked him, which one of the two celestial dancers was the better one of the two. The two dancers Rambha and Urvashi were equally beautiful, talented, and graceful and used to entertain at the court of Indra. That evening Indra noted with minute precision each move and expression of the two damsels as they danced together in unison, but he could not find a flaw in either. He turned to Narada to help him judge the better of the two.

Narada suggested a dance competition wherein musicians and accompanists were asked to play a myriad tunes of music from the slowest to the fastest. The contest went on for days, but neither of the two dancers did falter. Indra was at his wits end.

The following day when the contest entered the next round, Narada asked for four lotus buds to be brought to him. He touched each of them and then gave two each to both the dancing girls. So now both Rambha and Urvashi had a lotus bud in each of her hands and the music started. Narada instructed the musicians to play slow and soft music. As the hours passed he instructed the musicians to play faster and faster still. A time came when the Apsaras were dancing so fast that you could barely see their limbs as they whirled to the music, Narada signalled for the music to be sped up even further.

All of a sudden Rambha tossed one of the lotus buds away with a jerk! The musicians abruptly halted! Resultantly Urvashi became the winner of the contest!

"But, what happened to Rambha?" asked Indra. Narada smiled mischievously saying that he had touched the lotus buds and placed a black scorpion into each of them. While dancing, the girls were holding the flowers gracefully in their hands. As the music became faster and faster the stress increased. Rambha, in a moment of stress, squeezed her palm and the black scorpion inside bit her hard! She spontaneously jerked her hand and the flower got flung away!

The story has a deep meaning. Modern living has made our lives so fast, it's like we are always jet speeding and trying to accomplish ten things at a time. An average teenager in a metro city receiving a decent education in a college probably has access to a smart phone, Wifi, internet, email, Whats'app, snapchat and whatnot.

Each notification on his/ her phone, demands attention. The mind is expected to attend to and reply to all messages, jokes, forwards, photographs etc ... the list is too long to enumerate. An average office going person who has access to a computer or a laptop is also zig zagging between work related emails, internet surfing, linked-in, networking etc. etc.

Needless to say, stress levels are sky rocketing in everyone. Equanimity of mind is a rarity in the world today. From babies to oldies, it seems everyone is stressed. So, is it a wonder that the scorpion inside stings us? The world is not going to stop giving you stress. It is unreasonable to expect the world to be kind to you. If you want to help yourself, you have to be kind to yourself. Doing is important but sometimes in the process, the mental build up is so much that stress overpowers and everything comes crashing down.

29
A Drop of Blood!

"From birth to death, from dawn till night, man pursues fleeting pleasures by the exploitation, the despoiling, and the desecration of Nature, ignoring the truth that it is the property of God, the Creator, and any injury caused to it is a sacrilege which merits dire punishment."

A young man was blessed by a holy sage with an unusual boon. A single drop of his blood, if given to any one, could cure the recipient of any disease or illness. Anyone in his village, falling sick, would ask for a drop of his blood. Just a drop administered, would work the miracle of a perfect cure! The news of the wonder blood spread, people from neighbouring villages started coming in search of the man.

As years passed, the queue of visitors seeking his blood became unending. Each day from dawn to dusk the man was inundating sickly men and women with a single drop of blood each.

A day came when the man became frail and weak. It was becoming increasingly difficult for him to squeeze even a few drops of blood from his bruised hands. But the requests from people who had tasted blood were now turning into demands. Each person said, "It's just one drop that I need!" "At least spare a drop for me, I am going to die, if you don't." "Let me be the last one, but don't turn me away."

A time came when the wonder blood man was too weak to give any more. He was dying. But the serpentine queue outside his house was still thirsty and pleading for his blood.

Not a single person thought about how to save the dying healer. Each one thought only about himself.

Dear Reader, pause here for a moment to think. Who is the healer and forever-giving one?

It is the Earth! Yes, our very own, Mother Earth! Man has

unashamedly used and abused the Earth. He has poisoned it with chemicals, effluents, plastics,polythene and things suchlike. Man today is self-centred. He thinks only of himself. The indiscriminate use of the elements of nature, has caused so much ecological imbalance that nature is taking its revenge on man in the form of Earthquakes, tsunamis, floods, famines etc. The rate at which the elements are being polluted, one wonders what we will be able to pass on to the coming generations! Pure soil, pure and clean water and air ... These are what we need to give our children as inheritance. But will these be in a condition fit for human use, in times to come? I wonder ...

30

Little Sparrow

"Fully rely on the grace of God, earn it and keep it. Then whatever be the magnitude of the calamity you face, you can survive it without any harm."

This is a little anecdote that our Beloved Bhagwan Baba, once narrated to His students.

There was a huge tree in a forest. It had a huge trunk and many large branches. The branches further had numerous small branches growing on them and there were innumerable leaves on them all. A tiny sparrow was perched on one of the tender branches.

All of a sudden, a storm started to brew. First of all, the leaves of the tree started fluttering. As the wind became stronger, the lighter branches started shaking. Eventually the gale became a virtual tempest and the mighty trunk of the tree started to shake!

But what about the sparrow? Yes! This is what Bhagwan Baba asked His students as they sat around him, eagerly awaiting the climax of the story. He asked them, "What happened to the sparrow?"

The boys offered answers like, "It got badly hurt". Or, "It died!" But Baba shook His head, smiled and said "Nothing happened to it! It just flew away!" Now, that was quite a disappointing and a seemingly ordinary climax to a suspense filled build up. Baba said, "The tiny bird flew away because it was independent!"

It was 'in'-dependent! It was dependent on its own inner reserve of strength. It did not rely on the might of the tree to give it shelter or succor! In times of distress or crisis, look within for strength, before you reach out to others for help!

More often than not, you are self-sufficient to deal with the situation. It is just a question of looking within and having the faith that God's grace is eternally your legacy.

31

Tat Twam Asi

"Meditate upon your reality and always remember this fact: "Wherever I am, I am always Divine". Hold firmly to this belief. This is the truth contained in the scriptural proclamation Tat Twam Asi."

It is said that King Janaka once held a congregation of Sages. He asked them to give him the knowledge of the ultimate truth i.e. Atma jnana and do it in a minute! There was a large number of Rishis present but none of them took up the challenge of imparting the knowledge of the eternal truth to the king in just a minute's time span. There was a throne, lying vacant next to the King. The king said, “Whoever can enlighten me; I invite him to occupy this throne.”

Still no one came forward. Rishi Ashtavakara was a very learned sage who had been born with a body that was twisted in eight places, such that he could move around with great difficulty. He was also present in that august gathering. Slowly he got up and painfully made his way, step by step and ascended the vacant throne. Just as he occupied the chair, every one present, burst out laughing. Rishi Ashtavakara said calmly, “How sad it is for me to have come all the way to attend this congregation. I thought this would be a place where many learned men would be present. But alas! It seems this place is full of shoemakers only.” Now that was too much. The Rishis rose in indignation. How dare this twisted and crippled creature call us shoemakers! Ashtavakara continued, “The learned are able to see through to the Atma resident within the body. They do not get impressed or put off by the deformities of the physical encasement of the soul. It is the shoemaker who deals in skin. He takes a look only at the skin and its shape and form. It seems all of you can see only my skin, so you must be shoemakers; all of you!”

There was pin drop silence. King Janaka was very impressed. He said, “Oh, Venerable one! Can you give me the knowledge of the ultimate, here and now?”
The sage said, “That I can. But, you shall have to give me some Guru Dakshina in return for the knowledge.”

The king said, "I shall give you, whatever you want; whatever is there in my power to give!"
The sage smiled and said, "I too shall ask for only that, which I know is in your power to give!"
The king said, "I am ready. Ask for whatever you want."
The sage again confirmed from the king if his resolve to give was strong and sound. Then he said, "Oh king! Give me your *(tan-man- dhan)* body, mind and wealth!" The king paused for a moment and said, "I give you my body, mind and wealth."

As was the custom of the time, a handful of water was poured from the hands of the king to the hands of the Rishi and the transfer was completed virtually.

The sage said, "Oh Janaka, now come and sit down on the floor." That almost took everyone's breath away. But the king was a great soul. He quietly sat down on the floor in front of the Rishi. The Rishi said, "All your wealth, your palace and its riches, are mine. Don't think about them; turn your thoughts away from them." The king's mind flew to the queen, his family and his people. Then he realized that all that belonged to the Rishi now. He thought of his army, his kinsmen, but that too belonged now to the Rishi.

The king's mind flitted to and fro from this to that and the other, while the sage intently watched the changing expressions on his face. Finally, the king closed his eyes and withdrew his mind from everything and started understanding the truth. The Rishi whispered into the king's ear, "Tat Twam Asi!" (Meaning: That is who you are!) A few moments later, the Rishi asked the king, "Now, do you understand?" The king nodded slowly. Yes! He had understood the ultimate truth. He and God were in unison! The Atma and the Paramatma are one and the same!

32

Come Rain or Sun

"To get the attitude of surrender and dedication, you must have Faith in God. God, whose play this world is. See Him in the beauty, the grandeur, the order and the majesty of Nature."

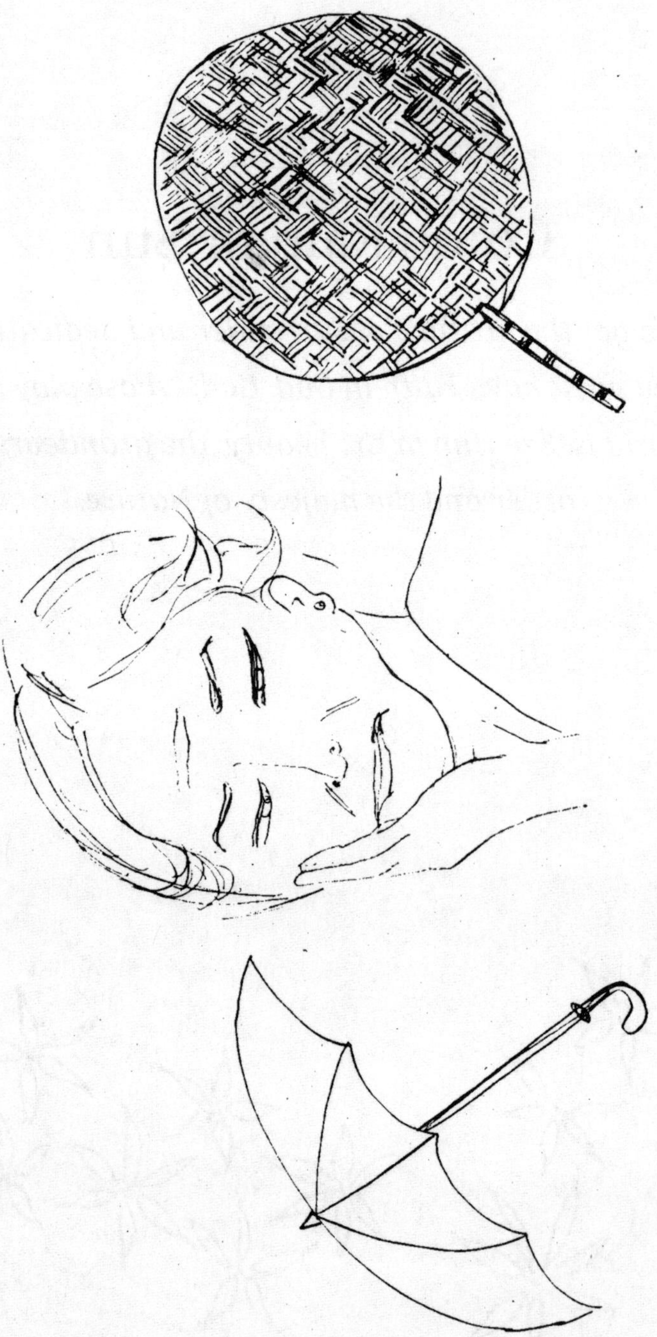

It was monsoon time when a young lad in Kerala noticed an old woman sitting in the park under the shelter of a canopy. It was raining heavily. The old woman had tears in her eyes. The young man asked the old woman, "Amma, why are you crying?" The old woman wiped away a tear and said, "Because it's raining so hard!" The youngster did not know what to say except, "Uh! Don't worry, it will stop soon."

The next day the fellow noticed the old woman sitting on a bench in the park, crying again. It was a sunny day and the fellow wiped the sweat off his brow as he asked her, "Amma, why are you crying again today?" The old woman closed her eyes to the blinding light of the sun and said, "Because the Sun is shining and it is so hot!"

The follow was puzzled. He asked the old woman, "What is there to cry about? The Sun shall set by the evening. Anyways, if it rains you cry and if it is sunny you cry too, what do you really want?"

The old woman said, "You see, my daughter is married to a man who makes hand-fans out of dried palm leaves. If it rains he doesn't sell a single fan so my daughter and her family go hungry. I feel sad for her, so I cry."

The boy asked, "But, why do you cry when the Sun shines?" The woman said, "My other daughter is married to a man who makes umbrellas. If the Sun shines brightly, he doesn't sell any umbrella and my daughter and her children go hungry so I cry for their bad luck!"

The young fellow smiled and said, "Amma, the day the Sun shines you should feel happy for your daughter who is married to the fan seller. And when it pours you should be happy for your daughter who is married to the umbrella seller!"

Isn't it true that we sometimes cry over silly things? We should try and look for reasons to smile. Come rain or sun, life is not always a bed of roses. But then each situation has a darker side as well as a brighter one. It is a matter of attitude or perspective. The choice is in your hands! Do you choose to cry or to laugh?

33

How Will I Die?

"The God of Death, Yama is also called Kaala, which means time. Time is the true God of Death. Time knows no mercy; you have to leave when the time is over."

A son was born to a renowned astrologer who was also a Minister in the King's palace. When he made his son's horoscope, the astrologer realized that the child was destined to die on a particular day at the age of six years by snake bite. This made him very sad, but he did not breathe a word of this to anyone, not even to his wife. The ill-fated day came and the astrologer sent a message to the king that he would not attend court that day. He told his wife to lie down on the bed on one side, whereas he himself lay on the other side. He put their son in the middle of the bed. He thought, a snake cannot climb on to a bed. If the child stays between us and does not get down, and if I can save him from snakebite at the time predestined for his death, then the child will live a long life. At the inopportune moment, a snake fell down from the ceiling, right in the middle of the bed and bit the child. The child died instantly. The snake slithered off. The astrologer was miserable but he followed the snake, he wanted to know more about destiny; this time, his own destiny! The snake entered a river. The man saw that the snake raised its hood over one side of a boat. Four men on the boat saw it and toppled over the other side of the boat due to fright. They drowned in the river and died. Meanwhile the snake climbed into the boat and bit the other two men on it. They too died. The snake moved on to land now. It moved into a street. Suddenly it took the shape of a beautiful woman. The woman befriended a rich merchant. She then treacherously stabbed the merchant to death and took his money away. The woman moved on, the bewildered astrologer followed its trail of death. The woman turned around and asked the astrologer, "Why are you following me?" He said, "I want to know who you are. I want to know why you keep on changing form. I want to know how I will die." The woman said, "I am death. I change form so that howsoever a person is destined to die, I don that form. Your son was destined to die by snake bite. The four men on the boat were destined to die due to drowning caused by fear of a snake. The other two were destined to die by snake bite and the merchant was destined to die because of his obsession for beautiful women." The man said, "Tell me how I will die." The woman said decisively, "That, I will not tell you." "Then I shall keep on following you," said the man obstinately. The man watched the woman change forms, from one to another. Eventually the woman said, "All right, you have followed me long enough. I will tell you. A crocodile will eat you while you are in water and you will die." The man went back to the King's palace and assumed his duties. Years later a son was born to the queen. The astrologer, after studying the horoscope of the new born prince, told the king that a prayer was to be performed for him or the child would die. The king told the astrologer to arrange for it. The astrologer said, "My Lord, the prayer has to be performed by someone, who stands in water and holds the baby boy in his arms and then offers water to the Sun God. I do not want to stand in water for I am destined to be killed by a crocodile. So I will find another priest to perform the prayer." The King said, "I don't have faith in any one else. I cannot afford to lose my son. I will get a lake made with a fully cemented floor. Purified water shall be filled in it. What to talk of crocodiles even a tiny fish will not be there in it."

So the astrologer agreed. An artificial lake was made and the astrologer stood in the water holding the prince in his arms and offered water to the Sun God. Just then the prince spoke, "Do you recognize me?" The astrologer said, "No." The prince said, "You eluded me for a long time. Eventually I had to take birth in the King's palace, to bring you to this situation. I am your crocodile!" The prince changed into a crocodile and devoured the astrologer! No one can run away from death. It lies only in God's hands.

34
A Splitting Headache

"The truth is shining inside you, waiting to be discovered. God is your Indweller and so when you seek Him outside, He cannot be caught. Look for Him within you."

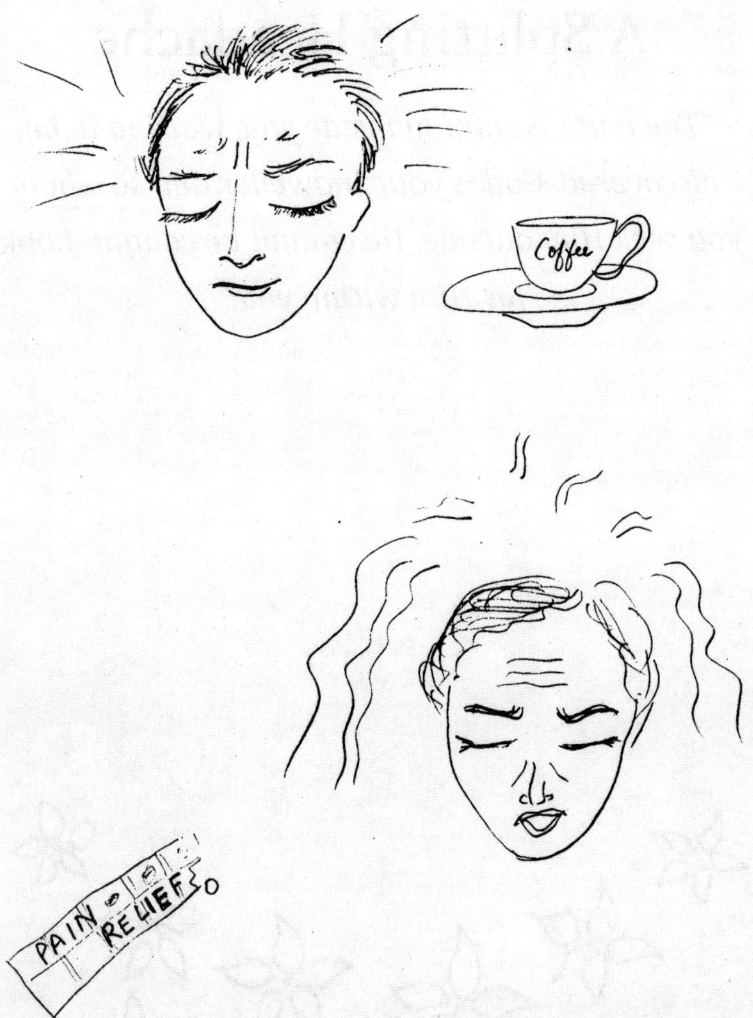
Coffee
PAIN RELIEF

The proprietor of a coffee shop had been busy all day. Being Saturday, it was very crowded and the customers were just unending. He had been on his toes since morning. Towards the evening he felt a splitting headache surfacing. As the clock ticked away, his headache worsened. Unable to bear it, he stepped out of the shop leaving his staff to look after the sales.

He walked across the street to the Chemist, to buy himself a painkiller to relieve his headache. He swallowed the pill and felt relieved. He knew that in a few minutes he would feel better. As he strolled out of the shop, he casually asked the salesgirl, "Where is Mr Savarkar (the Chemist)? He's not at the cash counter today!" The girl replied, "Sir, Mr Savarkar had a splitting headache and said he was going across to the coffee shop. He said a cup of hot coffee would relieve him of his headache."
The man's mouth went dry and he mumbled, "Oh! I see."

This is a typical case of looking outside ourselves for something that we have within us. How strange but true! The chemist relieves his headache by drinking coffee and the coffee shop owner finds relief in a pain relieving pill!

A man hunts across the lengths and breadths of the universe to find peace. Eventually he finds it in his heart and realizes that peace is really a state of mind. He undertakes many a pilgrimage to find God. Eventually he realizes that God is the in-dweller of the heart!

We asked our son Shiven, how he felt about being able to be in Parthi for Swami's 90th birthday. This is what he had to say...

The bliss of being in Prasanthi Nilayam on Swami's 90th Birthday

Ever since the start of this calendar year, the global Sai community has been buzzing with excitement in anticipation of the 90th Birthday of our most Beloved Lord. The social media team from Puttaparthi has been extremely efficient with their timely posts about all that goes on at Bhagawan's abode. From the most anticipated morning e-mail Sai Inspires from PrasanthiNilayam, to the live streams of programmes at the Sai Kulwant hall, to the video's on YouTube, and the posts on Facebook and Instagram; I love, enjoy and look forward to them all.

Another thing these posts do is make the heart long to go to Parthi to experience the feelings that are only felt when physically at that divine land. As November came, the thought of wanting to go to Parthi came to me and I shared it with my mother, hoping that Swami would somehow make it work. I had exams till the 16th of November, for which I'd spent months in preparation. I had been praying to Him for His blessings, but couldn't help but worry about the outcome. When I came home after the last one, my mother broke the news to me- "We are going to Parthi." I was pleasantly shocked and at a loss for words, the joy that I felt, how blessed I've felt since then, it's indescribable.

I feel that we keep worrying about our terrestrial and temporal wants and needs, while He takes care of us wholly, in a way that only He can. So why must we worry? To paraphrase from my favourite text, Swami's Prayer for Surrender, by worrying we demonstrate that we do not believe in His love for us, we prove that we do not consider our lives to be under His control and that nothing escapes Him.

As I ruminate about what to offer to Him on His birthday, inspiration dawns in His own words from the 90th Birthday Theme song*... *"Premaswaruplara! Happy happyhappy, Be Happy! Happy happy, Make others Happy! All will be happy, God will be happy!!!"*

Happy Birthday Dearest Lord!

Yours forever and always striving to make you happy!!!

Shiven Tandon

**https://soundcloud.com/radiosai/90th-birthday-theme-audio*

35

God's Routine

"Though God is omnipresent, He has to be discovered and cognised in order to experience the bliss."

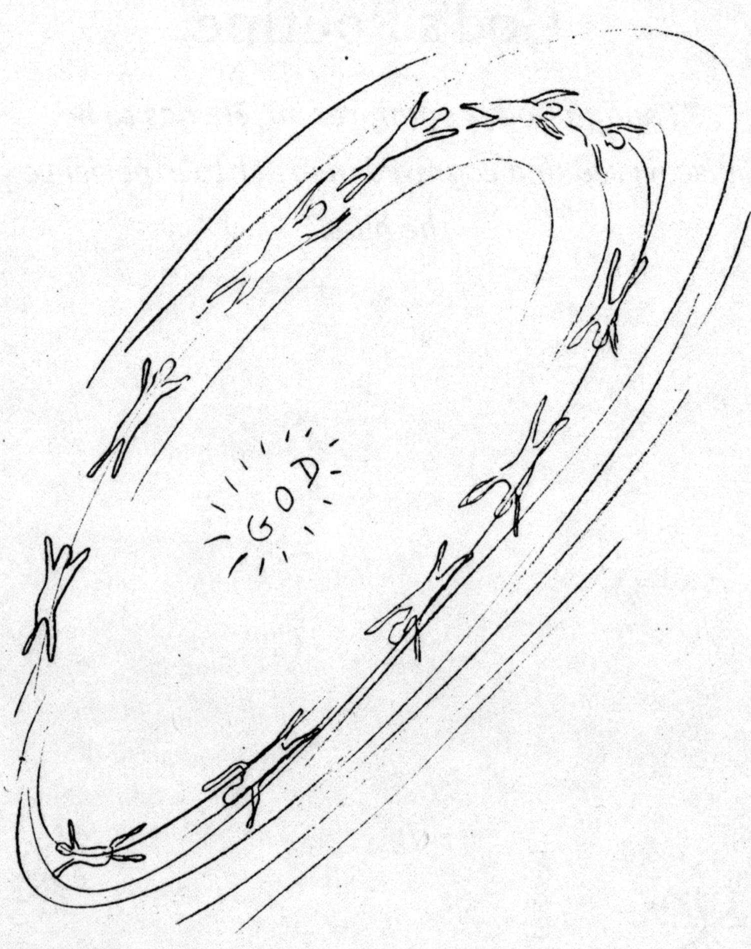
GOD

Our scriptures hold some amazing stories. This one is very meaningful. There was a king who was intelligent and fun loving. He had a court full of intelligent ministers because he loved discussions and debates on all kinds of topics.

One day, some questions sprang up in his mind and he told his Chief Minister that he wanted the answer to these questions. He also ordered that if the ministers were not able to answer his questions, they should leave the king's court and not return. The questions were – What does God eat? What does God do? Where does God live? When does God laugh?

No one could answer the questions. The infuriated king stomped out of court, dismissing all the Ministers and ordering the Chief Minister to go and look for someone who could answer these questions. The king further declared, "Who so ever is able to give the answers to my questions, shall be made the king and I shall gladly serve as his attendant."

The Chief Minister set off in search of such a wise man. He searched from village to village and town to town, but he could not find the right person. One day while he was very tired and distressed, he thought to himself, "If I go back without finding such a man, I would be failing in my duty and shall be the recipient of the king's wrath. I would be ridiculed and punished. So what should I do? Should I commit suicide? No! No! Why do discredit to all the good karma that I have earned? Why to waste this precious human life that I am blessed with? Oh, God! I have tried my best. Help me! I don't know what to do!"

Then God sent him a thought, "Since you have done everything to the best of your ability, even if you have not succeeded in completing the job, it is not your fault. Go back to the king ..." With this thought to comfort him and with prayers on his lips he started his return journey. On the way he was overcome by the heat of the afternoon sun and sat down under a mango tree to rest.

As he lay down to rest, he started humming a popular tune in praise of the Lord. A farmer, who was tilling his land, came and sat down by him. The farmer said, "You seem to be a Kshatriya. I am a Brahmin. This is my land. Since you are resting here, you are my guest. Come and share my lunch. Then if you like you can tell me your story. I can see that you are troubled by something." So the two men ate together and the Chief Minister told his tale of woe to the farmer. The farmer said, "I am greatly thankful to God for directing you to me. I am sure I can answer your king's questions. Please take me to him."
So, the two of them travelled for three days, to get to the King's court. The king seated the farmer on a fine chair and paid obeisance to him. The king asked his first question, "What does God eat?" The farmer said, "When man attains money, property, position, strength and power he becomes proud. In that state of mind, he commits many bad deeds. Then, God eats his pride! Since the beginning of creation, has anyone's name and fame remained forever? Ravana? Hiranyakashyapu? Shishupala? Duryodhana? Oh King! Look at your own Council of Ministers. Haven't you struck down their pride in a moment? Pride is the food of God. Just as a gardener looks after his garden but does not hesitate to chop off the branches of a tree that grow too much. He does not bat an eyelid, before plucking off the flowers

from a bush in full bloom!"

The king was very impressed by the answer. He was about to ask his next question when the farmer said, "Oh king! You are forgetting your promise." The king gladly seated the wise farmer on the throne and coroneted him King. He seated himself at the feet of the new King and asked, "What does God do?" The farmer-king said, "God turns a 'mountain into dust' and 'dust into a mountain', in a second; just by His sweet will. He turns 'a king into a pauper' and 'a pauper into a king!' Look at me, I am a poor farmer who earns his bread by the sweat of his brow and you are a King. But right now, I am a King and you are my servant! This is God's work! This is what He does!"

A stunned audience watched as the third question was asked, "Where does God live?" The farmer-king said, "God is present everywhere. He has countless names. The purpose of the Narasimha Avtar was to show that God is Omnipresent! To show to all present and to prove Bhakta Prahlada right, Lord Vishnu emerged out of a pillar in the court of King Hiranyakashyapu in the form of Narasimha. God lives everywhere! Show me a place where He is not present!"

The king was indeed in bliss. He asked his last question. "When does God laugh?" The farmer answered, "The soul is born and re-born again and again. Each time while in the womb of the mother, the unborn child prays and begs God for deliverance from the hell of the tiny womb it is caged in. Then God makes him promise, "I will not forget you Lord. I will always remember you. Please give me one more chance." In this way the unborn child begs God to give him a chance to be born and get out of the womb. He promises to be good in his new life. But as soon as the jiva is born, he forgets all his promises and gets entangled in the worldly and mundane. This is when God laughs!

The answer was so satisfying that the king fell at the feet of the farmer-king. But the farmer said, "Oh King! I am a Brahmin. I cannot rule this Kingdom. It is yours. Remember that God is immanent in everything in the universe. Each person in your Kingdom is an embodiment of God. The food that your people eat is eaten by God. If they are happy, God is happy. Don't forget that!"

36

The Spider in a Hurry

"Every human being has the capacity to seek and secure the Truth of the Universe of which they are a part of; they have the wherewithal to train themselves in virtue, justice, love and sympathy to escape from the particular to the Universal."

During the Mahabharata war that lasted for 18 days, Sage Vyasa went through untold agony because both the parties to the war, i.e. the Pandavas and the Kauravas were of his lineage and he was attached and bonded to them all. He could not muster the strength to bring himself to watch this fratricidal carnage.

One day as he hastened past the battle field where another day of bloodshed was about to begin, he saw a spider scurrying speedily across the ground. The sage asked the spider, "What's the hurry? Where are you off to?"

The spider hurried to the other side of the road and up an anthill where he felt he was safe. Having perched himself on the anthill he replied panting, "Don't you know that the chariot of Arjuna is going to pass this way soon. If I get caught under its wheels, I shall be crushed to death! But now I am safe!" The sage was highly amused. He laughed aloud and said, "So what if you were to be ground to a paste under the wheels of the chariot of the mighty Arjuna? Who would even bother to shed a tear? No one would even bother to look twice!"

Now that volley of words, hit the spider worse than an arrow from Arjun's bow. He was enraged and said angrily, "What do you know, Oh insolent sage? You men have such bloated egos that you do not bother to look beneath. You think that if you die, this world shall suffer a great loss; and if I die, I shall not be missed at all! I too have a wife and children. I have parents and a home where I store food. I also know the feelings of love, hate, anger, hunger, happiness, sadness, loneliness and the agony of losing a loved one. The world belongs as much to me, as it does to you!"

The sage hung his head in shame and walked away thinking, "Saamaanyam path pasubhir naraani." (For man and beast, these things are common.) This is the realization, the liberation, the illumination, the revelation! "Sarvam Vishnumayam Jagath!" (The whole world is filled with God!)

Then it dawned on him that besides the feelings or things that are common to men and animals, there are certain others that only man is blessed with. Amongst all of God's creation, it is only man who is blessed with the faculty to enquire into the ultimate. The yearning for truth, beauty, goodness and the awareness of the underlying unity and Divinity in all creation, these attributes of wisdom are the unique treasures that belong only to man!

37
Destiny

"Charity is the true ornament of the hand (Hasthasya bhushanam daanam). Your hands are useless if they do not perform acts of charity. Do not worry about ups and downs, loss or gain, joy or grief. You are the creator of your own destiny."

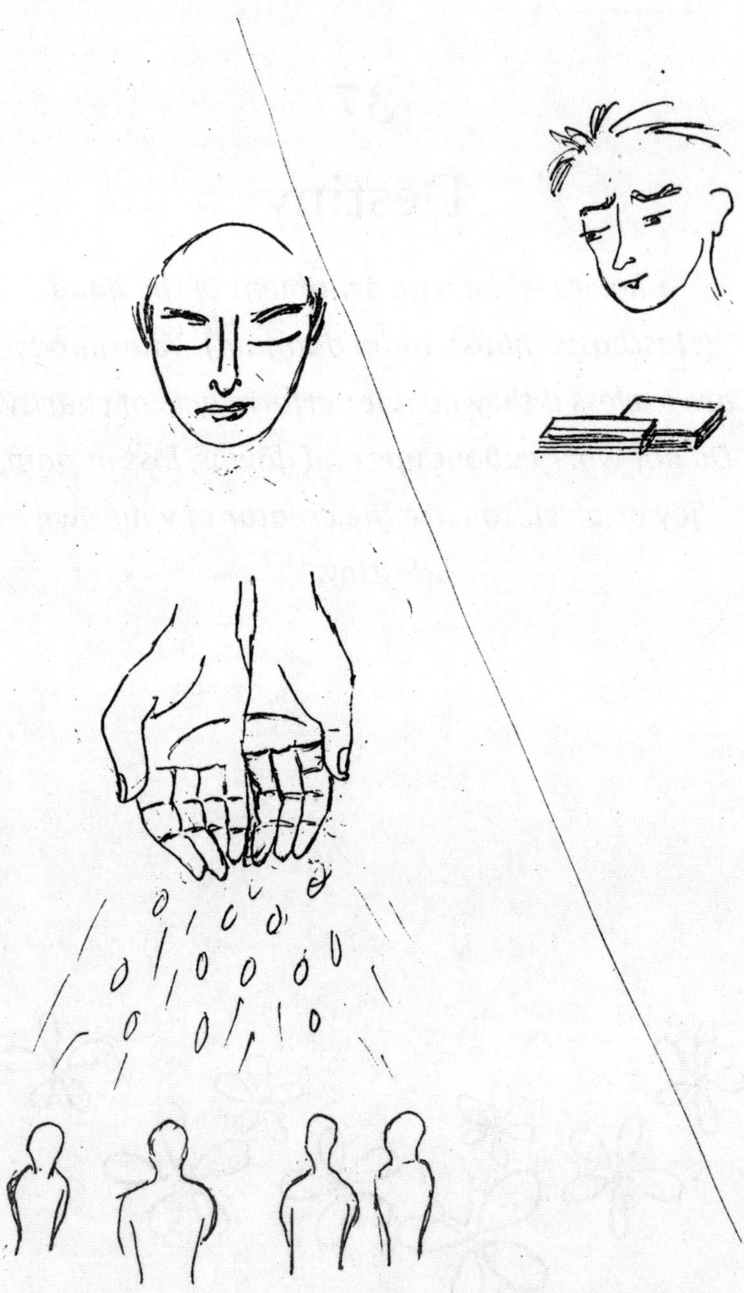

There once were two brothers. One of them was a miser, but the other one was a philanthropist. A wise man visited their house one day. They looked after the wise man well and made him comfortable. While leaving, the wise man was very pleased with their hospitality and blessed them profusely. He asked each of them if they had anything to wish for.

The miser said, "Please bless me so that whatever the Lord has destined for me, I should keep getting proportionately all my life, so that I can live comfortably till my last day. My needs are few and I spend wisely. But sometimes I fear for the future. When I am old, I may not be earning, so who will look after me?"

The wise man blessed him and said, "So be it! You shall always have enough for yourself. You shall never be left wanting!" He then turned to the philanthropist, who said, "Oh wise one! Please ask the Lord Almighty to give me all at once, whatever He has destined for me in this life. I would rather have it all together and do what I really want to, rather than keep waiting for the good things all my life!"

The wise man said, "As you please, my child."

Within a few days, the philanthropist brother had huge profits from business, he won a great sum of money in a lottery, and an aunt left him a huge estate in her will. In few words, let's say, it was not just raining, it was pouring wealth from all quarters.

This man gave away huge amounts to charity. He also made tremendous investments in business. He gave generous gifts to his friends and relatives. His policy as before was give, give and give yet again! His business gave unprecedented returns and more money continued to pour in.

The miser brother on the other hand, continued his life as a simpleton. The miser met the wise man one day and asked him, "Oh wise one! You said my brother would get everything destined for him all at once, but his good luck seems to be never ending. I don't get it."

The wise man said, "I gave him, whatever was predestined for him. Now, he is reaping the dividends of his good deeds. That is a bonus! It's not planned. But through his habits of empathy and sympathy he has changed his destiny!"

38
The Colloquium

"When a cold bit of coal is placed in the midst of glowing cinders, and when the fire is fanned, the coal too starts glowing with the fire. The Jnaana Agni or the Fire of Wisdom operates similarly."

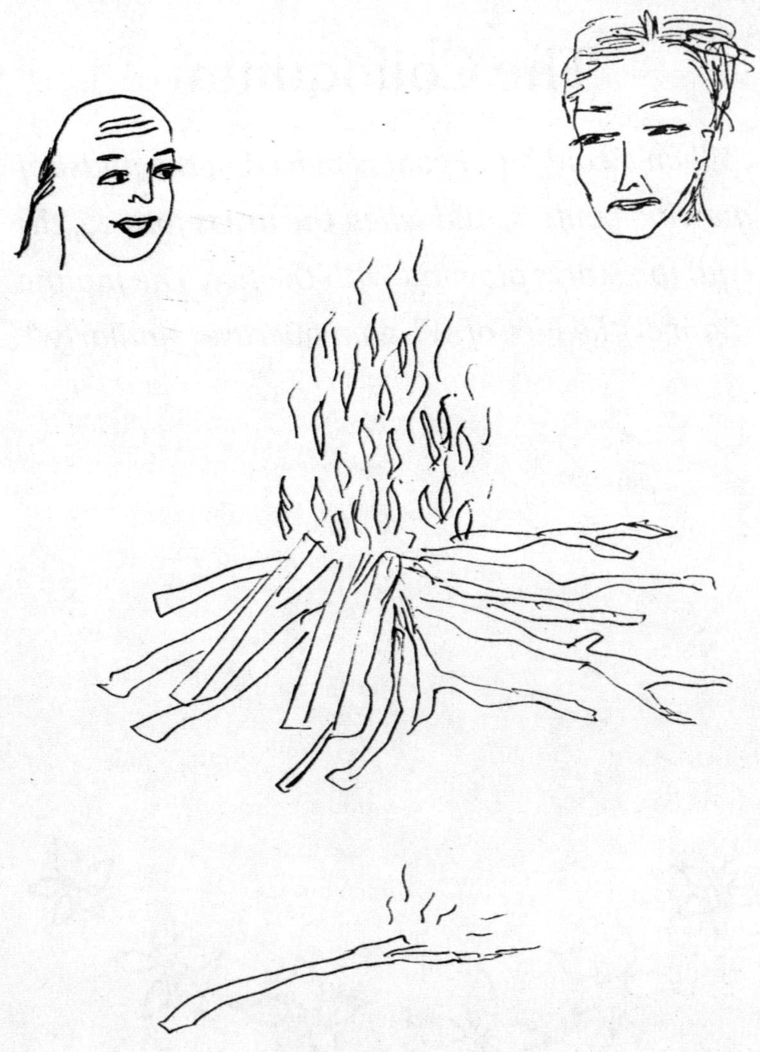

Prakhar was a middle aged man who was a regular visitor at the local temple. He would participate in the morning Aarti almost every day. He would take keen interest in the day to day activities of the temple. One day he felt that he was wasting his time in these activities and anyways, he thought, God is everywhere. So he might as well stay at home and worship Him as and when he pleased. So, he stopped going to the temple.

The priest at the temple took note of Prakhar's absence in the coming days. A week went by and then a fortnight. The priest decided to find out if all was well with this ardent devotee of the Lord. So, after completing his routine for the day, the priest closed the temple and went to Prakhar's house. It was a chilly night and Prakhar was enjoying a log fire in the backyard. The fire burnt merrily as the cool wind swished across the courtyard. The priest sat near Prakhar, they exchanged a nod of recognition, but neither of them spoke a word. The priest watched as Prakhar seemed to be engrossed in his own thoughts. After a while, the priest got up and picked out a half burnt piece of wood from the bonfire.

He placed the wood a little away from the fire. After a while the orange flame from that piece of wood started dying out. The wind managed to extinguish it by and by. Prakar noticed this, from the corner of his eye, but spoke nothing.

Some more time passed. The priest picked up the half burnt piece of wood and put it back into the crackling fire. It started burning merrily again. The priest quietly went away.

Come morn and Prakhar was present at the morning Aarti, as

punctual as he had always been.

A single man is not always able to do things as efficiently as a group is. In this case too, the routine of going to the temple and being a part of the colloquium of people, attending all events etc. play their own part in establishing a connection with God. The Hindus spend a lot of time in decorating their shrines, singing the praises of the Lord, going on pilgrimages and the like. Some people wonder, why so much time is spent in such activities? During the long hours spent in such things, if one is able to connect with the Lord even for a split second, one gets a feel of Divinity that is unexplainable through the medium of the twenty six alphabets.

The chances of experiencing Divinity, increases manifold when one is with a group of people, trying to reach out to God. The prayers of all collectively become a potent force and each one is benefitted so many times over! It is always advisable to be a part of a group of likeminded seekers of God.

Just as a cricketer needs a team to play with, a musician needs a band or a child needs a group of playmates, each one of us needs the tug of a divine peer group to spur us into the flowing stream of Godliness. Each one derives strength and support from all others in the group.

39

One Vice or Hole

"Young people should get rid of bad thoughts and habits. The spiritual quest cannot be put off to old age."

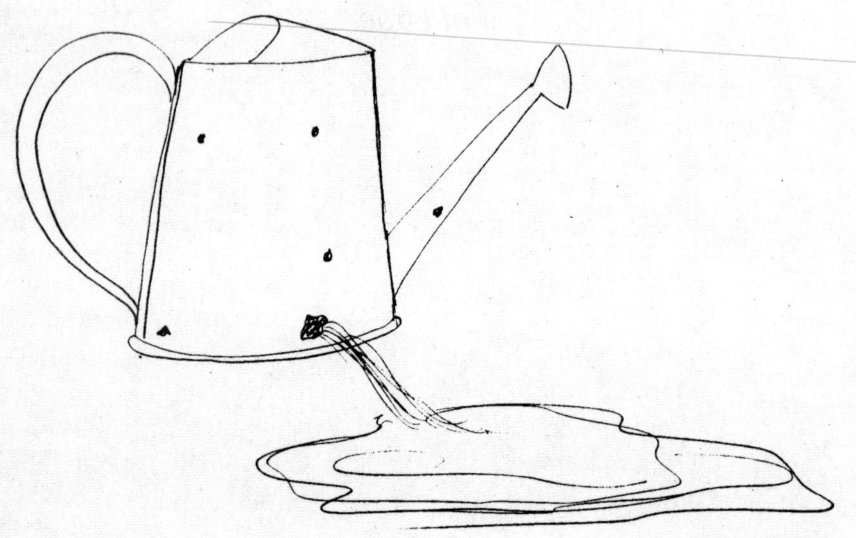

In an orthodox Hindu family, a father noticed his son of fifteen, smoking. The boy would try and slip away from his father's attention when he smoked. The boy was otherwise a conscientious boy who was responsible towards his academics and sports too. Father decided that since the boy was performing well on all other fronts, it would perhaps be unwise to pull him up on this one vice. Given time, the vice would probably die its own death.

With the passage of time the boy started having irregular sleep patterns and his appetite went away too. He would not be able to eat his meals at the right time and would sometimes feign a headache or an upset tummy to avoid a confrontation with his father at the dining table. Mood swings and irritable temperament became a part of his character. The boy was now grown and at the threshold of his career. Father noticed that the boy's room smelt of cigarettes all the time and his health seemed to be deteriorating.

Finally, father asked him the question that he had been avoiding for a number of years now. "Son," he asked, "How many cigarettes do you smoke in a day?" "Huh?" asked the son distractedly. Father repeated his question. The young fellow said, "What? I don't smoke Dad. What makes you think I do?" But father saw the blood rushing to his son's cheeks. He said, "Son, you are a grown up man now. Let's talk like friends. Come on, out with the truth now." The lad hesitated, then said plainly, "Forty odd ..." Father's jaw dropped. He didn't expect this. He took a deep breath and continued, "For how long has this been going on?" The boy said, "Pretty long, I don't really remember." Father said, "You had all the right habits, what went wrong, why did you get into this? I can see that you are now not able to concentrate on your work. You do not eat or sleep well. Your mother and I are worried about you." The boy shrugged his shoulders and said, "Everyone has vices nowadays. I have just one. I don't steal, abuse, tell lies. I don't do drugs. Come on Dad, I'm human. Let me enjoy this one fancy that I have. Just leave me alone."

Father realized that there was no use counselling. The boy was not a kid any more. He was a man. A few days later, father was out gardening. The neighbour's little son was trying to plug the holes in a rusted old watering can, so that he could water the flower pots at the rear end of the driveway. By the time he would reach the flower pots with his can, the water would drain away from the numerous holes. The boy succeeded in plugging all the holes with an adhesive, except one, because this one was too big. As the little fellow struggled with his job, the man's son stood watching him, lazing on the other side of the fence. He said, "Hey! Little boy, unless you plug all the holes the water shall drain away. If the number of holes is less, the pace of the water loss shall be slower, but drain away it must."

The father stood behind his son and said softly. 'That's what I said too, my boy, one hole is enough to empty the barrel. When are you going to plug it?"

40
Be Careful What You Eat

"To dwell on God, one should be vigilant about the food and drink consumed by both - the body and the mind."

On numerous occasions Bhagwan Baba has explained the need of Paaka Shudhi (purity of the food being cooked), Chitta Shudhi (Purity of the mind of the cook) and Bhaanda Shudhi (purity of the vessel used for cooking). Bhagwan tells us of a young Sanyasi at Rishikesh, who had embraced asceticism at a very tender age. The boy was earnest in his devotion and committed to his resolve. One night he had a dream of a sixteen year old girl who cried before him. The dream repeated itself every consecutive night till the young boy was at his wits end for what to do.

He brooked the subject with his Guru, who asked him how long this had been going on and from where the lad had eaten food in these days. After investigating the matter, the Guru came to the conclusion that a sixteen year old girl had been married off by her father, much against her wishes to an old man. In frustration the girl committed suicide. The father performed her last rites as per the Hindu customs. On the thirteenth day of her death, the father had fed some Brahmins. This young Brahmin lad was one of those who had eaten there. The traumatized feelings of the old father and the distraught soul of the girl were imminent in the food served there. The emotions of the girl had crept into the boy and were troubling him. The guru taught the boy prayer and meditation to free him from the disturbed soul of the girl and also prayed for the departed soul to find peace and salvation.

With the grace of the Guru, the dream stopped repeating itself and the lad regained his peace of mind.

Here, Swami tells us that it is important to eat from places where the food is pure in all respects. However, it may not always be under our control to know about the cook and the cleanliness factors etc. for all of us have to eat out at social gatherings etc. So a simple solution to this problem is to offer the food to God, before partaking of it. How does this help? When we offer the food to God and He partakes of it, it becomes a Prasadam. Hence all impurities of all kinds are removed from it!

In this context Swami elaborates by citing an incident from the Mahabharata war. Towards the end of the war, Grandsire Bheeshama Pitamaha was lying wounded on a bed of arrows and blood was streaming out of his body, down the arrows into the ground. The Pandavas were gathered around their beloved Pitamaha and he was teaching them the importance of Dharmic rule. As Bhishama was preaching this, Draupadi who stood a few paces away, laughed ... At this Bheeshma asked her the reason for her contemptuous laugh.

Draupadi replied, "Oh! Venerable one! You preach the great principals of Dharma to my husbands who are verily the embodiments of Dharma and Truth. You, despite being the Patriarch of the Kuru clan, chose to remain silent when I was being disrobed by the evil Kauravas. Where was your so called Dharma at that time? How can YOU now preach Dharma?"

It was then that Bheeshma said with tears running down his aged eyes. "Yes Draupadi! You are right. I knew everything and yet did not come to your rescue. I had been eating the food cooked in the kitchen of the Kauravas for many years. That food deluded my intelligence; it even blurred my inner vision by casting a veil on it. But now, Arjuna's arrows have pierced my body and the dirty, contaminated blood has drained out of me. I repent that incident with all my heart. Now, that my good thoughts have surfaced and I can think with a pure heart, I give this lecture on Raj-Dharma to your husbands!"

These anecdotes stress upon the importance of a healthy mind in a healthy body. And the role of healthy and pure food in it!

41

The Strength of a Woman's Character

"The mansion of human life should be built on charity, purity, unity and Divinity. Women play a crucial role in cultivating these four pillars."

There is a legend about a Brahmin called Kaushik. He was a characterless man who contracted leprosy seemingly due to his habits and loose character. But his habits did not change. His wife Sumathi was a woman of great virtue and character. Due to the physical condition of Kaushik the couple was shunted out of the village and were living under a tree on the outskirts of the village. The virtuous Sumathi did not fail in performing her duties towards her diseased husband. One day Kaushik asked his wife to take him to a prostitute. Sumathi tried in vain, to dissuade him but the characterless man did not relent. So, Sumathi put her husband in a basket and carried him on her head and took him to a prostitute. The prostitute was stunned at this act of Sumathi. She gave a good piece of her mind to Kaushik and told him to go away.

Sumathi carried Kaushik on her head and took him back. She had to make her through a cremation ground in the darkness of the night.

Sage Mandavya had been falsely accused of stealing some money that had been left near him by a thief while running away. Mandavya was wrongly punished and was made to carry a huge stone around his neck. While he was carrying the burden of the heavy stone round his neck, he too was passing through the cremation ground at night.

As Sumathi inadvertently crossed by Sage Mandavya, the leg of Kaushik that was protruding out of the basket on her head, hit Mandavya and he cursed in pain. Mandavya said, "Who is it, who dares strike me with his foot? Oh insolent one! May your head break the moment the sun rises!!!" Sumathi begged

Mandavya to withdraw the curse, and spare the life of her husband. But Mandavya refused to let up.

Then Sumathi took a vow, "If I am a woman of character, then the Sun shall not rise!" Such was the power of this chaste woman, that there was no Sunrise and the world was steeped in darkness. Everyone prayed to Brahma. Brahma advised them to ask help from Anusuya the wife of Rishi Atri, for Anusuya was a woman of chastity.

Anusuya persuaded Sumathi to let the Sun rise, promising her that as soon as Kaushik died at sunrise, Anusuya would resurrect him. Anusuya kept her promise and gave Kaushik back, not only his life but also a disease-free body.

Women are capable of great things. They have great strength of character. The changing values of society today have set different dimensions for women and their role in the contemporary world. But deep down somewhere, the ancient values still hold true and are always a guiding light when in doubt.

42

The Dharmic Bear

"Dharma destroys the one who violates it.
Dharma also protects the one who protects it."

This is a story that most adults may have read in their childhood. But the lesson learnt is so pertinent that we feel it still is prudent to add it to this compendium.

A man went to a jungle in search of wild herbs. Dusk fell and all of a sudden he was confronted with a lion. The man started running for dear life. The lion chased him till the man succeeded in climbing up a huge tree. But what did he see! A bear was sitting on one of the upper branches of the tree. The man looked down to see the lion snarling up at him and looked up to see the bear staring down at him. He was caught between the devil and the deep sea. The lion called out to the bear, "Oh Brother! You and I are co-habitants of the jungle. Push this fellow down. I am hungry. I want my prey. Please help me."

The bear said calmly, "Sorry my friend, this tree is my home. This man is a guest in my home. It is against the ethics of guest relations to push him out of my home." The lion pleaded with the bear, but the bear was a principled creature and did not relent.

After a while, the bear went off to sleep. The man was utterly frightened and could not get a wink of sleep. The lion hovered around the tree restlessly. Seeing that the bear was sleeping, the lion whispered to the man, "I am hungry. It doesn't matter to me whether I eat you or the bear. Do me a favour, push the sleeping bear down. I shall eat it and go away. Then you shall be free to go home."

The thankless man did not think twice. He pushed the bear down. The sleeping bear woke up with a start and yelped in shock. Somehow, it was able to grab a branch in mid-air, before he dropped to the ground. Slowly but surely, the bear pulled himself up and secured a place on the tree. The lion said, "This worthless man forgot your goodness towards him. Now you should push him down to teach him a lesson. I am dying of hunger!" The bear said, "He did what his true nature is. But I shall stick to my innate nature. I cannot do it!"

The bear did not give up his Dharma! Today how easily we give up our Dharma for petty gains! It is never easy to do your duty, but do it, you must!

43

Lion or the Lame Fox

"If you choose to remain inactive, it is an indication of Thamoguna (quality of sloth and inaction leading to ignorance)! That is even worse than Rajoguna."

An ascetic went into the forest to meditate. He was always worried about his food and sustenance. One day he saw a lion killing a deer. The lion ate some of it and left the rest. As soon as the lion left, a lame fox came and ate the deer flesh. When the fox limped away, there came some vultures that pecked at every shred of flesh and cleaned up the skeleton. The ascetic thought, "The lame fox and the vultures got their food without having to work for it. God takes care of every one of His creatures. So why should I bother about my food and waste my time looking for it. I should spend my time in meditation and God shall arrange to send my food to me."

So, the ascetic sat in a cave to meditate. Time and again he would feel the pangs of hunger and would open one eye to check if the food had arrived, but nothing edible seemed to be coming his way. When he could bear the pangs of hunger no longer, he prayed to God, "Oh Lord! Do you love the lame fox and the vultures more than you love me? Do you care for them more? Won't you send me some food? I am going to die of Hunger."

Then God said, "My child! Why do you want to be like the lame fox or the vultures? Be like the lion. Work for your food; earn it by your efforts. And don't forget to save some for giving to others in charity. That is the right thing to do. You are healthy and strong, get up and get going!"

Laziness never gets us anywhere. It is up to us. Do we want to be like the self-reliant lion or the vultures or the lame fox?"

We asked our eldest son Saraansh, how he deals with the physical absence of Swami, in the present day. This is what he had to say...

Keep your head up for Sunrays

Whether you're troubled with your work, health, love, spirit or anything else, there is nothing that faith can't solve.

The only thing God expects from you is your unwavering faith towards him. It doesn't matter what God you believe in, because the concept of faith transcends religion and humanity.

It starts from within and empowers from within. If you've got enough faith, there is nothing that can't be fixed. Believe in yourself and your God, for he has given you the toughest of tasks since you have the capability to withstand what stands in the way. Don't give in to weakness, be steadfast, be stubborn on your goal and very soon it'll be in the palm of your hands. God gives His hardest battles to His strongest soldiers.

Saraansh Tandon

44
King vs God

"Leaving everything to His will is truly the highest form of devotion and the easiest way to win His Grace."

King Sundaravadanan ruled the Kingdom of Kannakpuri. There is an anecdote about how he got converted from an atheist to a firm believer of God.

The king often walked through the streets of the city to get a feel of the common man's life. One such night, he heard two beggars praying quite audibly. One of them invoked the grace of God. The other prayed for the grace of the King. The king had both beggars brought to his court the next day. The King asked both of them why they were praying as they were.

The first one said, "Oh king! I believe that God is the Lord and master of everything. He protects and sustains us all. If He showers grace on me, what more can I ask for?"

The second one said, "The king is the instrument of God. He is visible here and now. Who knows where God lives or if he listens to our prayers or not? If the king is pleased and showers his grace, what more can I ask for?"

The beggars left, but the king lost his peace of mind trying to find out which one of them was right. He discussed the matter with his Minister. The Minister opined that the beggar asking for God's grace was more sensible, but the egoistic king thought otherwise.

A few days later it was the King's birthday and he announced that gifts would be distributed to everyone in the city. On the said date, people lined up at the palace and the king gave fruits, vegetables and clothes to all. Around noon time the second beggar (the one who sought the grace of the King) stood in front of the King with his palms extended. The king recognized him. Quickly he signalled to his attendant and a special pumpkin was given to him along with an expensive silk robe. That day passed.

A few days later, the king went into the city again. He saw the same beggar sitting on the road side, begging for alms. The King questioned him, "After receiving the grace of the king, why are you still begging. Where is the pumpkin I gave you?" The beggar replied, "Oh King! I could not possibly have consumed such a huge pumpkin all alone. So I sold it for three annas."

The king exclaimed, "You fool! I had that pumpkin stuffed with gold and precious stones. You did not even bother to cut it open! If you had done so, you would have been a rich man."

The bewildered beggar stared in disbelief as the king walked away, shaking his head in disgust.

A short distance away the king saw a rich man wearing silken clothes and lots of ornaments. Two attendants flanked him as he walked. The King happened to see the man's face closely and exclaimed, "Your face seems familiar. Who are you? You are the beggar, who prayed for God's grace, aren't you? Are you really a rich man or a beggar?"

The man said, "Oh King! I am a rich man who was a beggar till a few days back. It was the death anniversary of my late mother and I had to feed seven Brahmins, so I bought a large pumpkin for three annas, to cook a meal for them. But, when I cut it open, I was amazed to find that it was full of diamonds, pearls, gold etc. By the grace of God, I am a rich man now. I don't need to beg anymore."

So whose grace are you going to ask for now? The king's grace or God's grace?

45

Did You See a Deer?

"You cannot always oblige, but you can speak always obligingly."

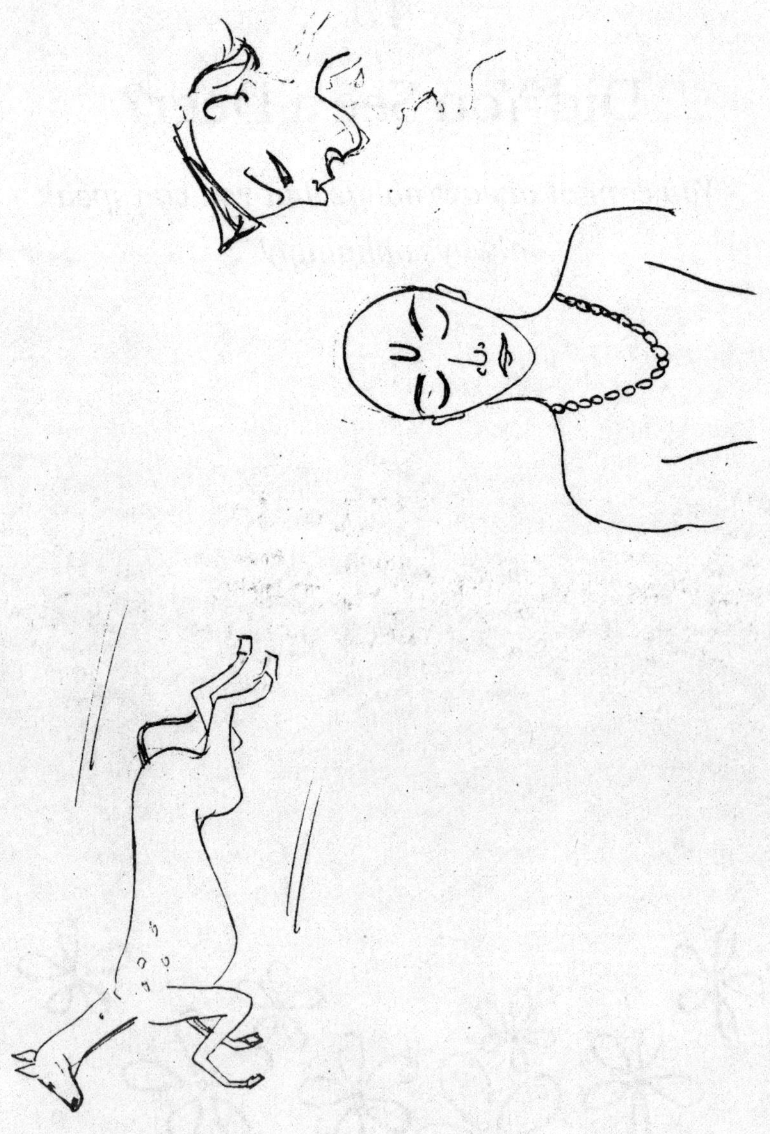

A hermit was meditating in a jungle. He heard the sound of an animal running and opened his eyes to see a deer whizzing past. Moments later, a hunter followed with a bow and arrow in his hand. He saw the hermit and quickly asked him. "Did you see a deer run this way?"

Here the hermit was faced by a dilemma ... a dharam sankat! If he told the hunter that he saw a deer go by that way, the hunter would surely catch up and kill the poor animal. If he said that he did not see any deer go by, he would be telling a lie. What to do now?

So, the hermit gave a very diplomatic answer. He said, "The ones that saw, cannot speak and the one that can speak, did not see." So saying he closed his eyes to resume his meditation. The perplexed hunter ran from here to there but was unable to find the deer, which had by then, gone off into the thickets.

Technically speaking, the hermit did not tell a lie. The eyes saw, but they could not speak and the mouth that could speak, did not see! In so doing the hermit spoke the truth; did his duty in protecting a living being; worked for the cause of peace; showed his love for God's creation and also practiced non-violence. Here do you think the thought of any kind of gratitude from the deer would have crossed the mind of the hermit? No! He just did what he did in the pay-it-forward circle of life!

This one act afforded him the opportunity to live out each of the five human values of Sathya, Dharma, Shanti, Prema and Ahimsa.

Bhagwan Baba says, "Once you see the world as the stage for His play, then you will no longer be misled, nor distracted, nor deceived by any tricks or stage effects."

Many a time we too are faced with such like situations. A mind surrendered and connected to God can give birth to a brainwave that succeeds in saving the situation. "Devotion," says Bhagwan Baba "is a way of life. It is not a uniform to be worn on special occasions."

If a person decides to live his life such as never to hurt anyone by his thought, word or deed, God surely gives him the strength and helps him live out his resolve.

46

The Richness of the Poor and the Poorness of the Rich

"Many millionaires today are engaged in filling their own belly. They are not prepared to give even a morsel of food as alms to a beggar who stands at their doorstep. What is the use of having such rich men in our country? They are rich only for name's sake but in reality they are the poorest of the poor."

In a que where food was being distributed to people who were rendered homeless due to Earthquake, stood a girl who like others had not had a decent meal for days now. She was the last one in the que and after giving her a packet of food, the good Samaritans moved off to the next camp. A moment later, came an old man who despite trying to hobble fast, could not make it in time. As the distribution van moved off, the girl saw that the old man, wiped a tear from his eyes. Without a second thought the girl opened her packet of food and said, "Come Baba, eat this food." The old man looked at her through hazy eyes and stared at her as if he had seen an angel. He said, "No, I can't take that; you must be hungry too." The girl insisted, so eventually the girl and the old man shared the food and smiled in contentment.

Meanwhile the van reached another devastated area, where there were people in the same condition. The area was supposed to have been a posh one, but it had been completely mowed down by the earthquake. There was a girl in the que for a food packet who the man handing out packets seemed to recognize. He asked her, "Who are you, young lady?" The girl spoke a little hesitatingly, "I am Ira ... daughter of Brijesh Lal." The man said, "Oh! Brijesh Lal was a very rich man! So did all of your family perish in the earthquake?" "No," she said. "Where are they?" The wistful look in her eyes touched his heart as she said softly, "My father and I were buried under the rubble. My father was a man of repute; a rescue team came to look for us, but my mother told them, that only she and my brother were there and that there was no one else when the calamity took place. So they took both of them to a safe place. I kept calling out, but no one heard me. My father was already dead. The next day another rescue team came. They saw me breathing and dug me out."

"Did you not tell them who you are? How could your mother do that?" The girl lowered her eyes and whispered, "It would be of no use. She never got along with my father. My mother was his first wife ... and now ..." The girl could speak no longer; and the man was at a loss for words too.

Isn't it amazing? Those who had nothing were able to value the priceless! Generosity in its true sense does not evolve within us when we have lots to give; its sprouts when we think of all as ONE and therefore do not have the urge to grab. Isn't life just a journey from I to We?

Strangely, sometimes the rich can be so poor ... and the poor can be so rich!

47
The Missing Shoes

"Practice moderation in speech for most misunderstandings and factions arise out of carelessly spoken words. When the foot slips, the wound can be healed. But when the tongue slips, the wound it causes in the heart of another will fester for life."

Tamang and Kapin were two brothers who had a shoe shop. They had a couple of old and faithful craftsman, who specialized in hand made shoes. For many years these brothers had a monopoly in the local shoe market. Their handmade Chinese shoes were comfortable and durable too. One day, ten pairs of trendy brown leather moccasins were delivered by the head craftsman at the shop counter. They were made of snake leather and were quite expensive.

Tamang had gone out for the day and Kapin was looking after the shop. Just before closing time, a customer bought a pair of the latest trendy brown moccasins. Soon Kapin closed the shop and went home. The following day was Kapin's weekly day off and Tamang opened the shop in the morning. He saw the new lot of shoes standing smartly at the counter. He happened to read in the stock register that ten pairs of shoes had been delivered. The sales register said that one pair had been sold at 8 pm. But the counter had only eight pairs on it.

The following day Tamang asked his brother Kapin if he had forgotten to enter the sale of the missing pair into the sales register, or had he liked it so much that he had taken a pair for himself?

Kapin looked puzzled and replied that he had sold only one pair and he had not taken any for himself. Tamang got annoyed and said sarcastically, "Well I guess then a ghost entered into those shoes and walked away with them!"

With each passing day, there was an increment in bickering and mistrust between the brothers. Soon the brothers came to such a juncture that they decided to split the business and Kapin offered to move out. He set up another shop across the road.

Eighteen years later, a gentleman walked into Tamang's shop and said, "My friend, are you the proprietor here?" "Yes, I am," said Tamang. "Have you been here for the last eighteen years?" "Sure," replied Tamang in surprise. "My friend, I have come here to make a confession. Eighteen years ago I came to this shop to look for a cheap pair of shoes, for mine was worn out beyond repair. You were at the rear end of the shop attending to a customer. At the counter were some expensive leather moccasins. I was desperate because my feet were so cold. I picked up a pair, slopped my feet into them and rushed out. But the guilt of the theft has haunted me all these years. I have come to confess and also to pay for them, for today I can afford to do so."

Tears welled up in Tamang's eyes as realisation dawned on him. He said, "The man with the customer was not me, but my brother. Please come with me to the shop across the road and repeat your story. That shall be payment enough."

The man went across to Kapin's shop and repeated his story. He was amazed to see Kapin come out of the shop to hug a sobbing Tamang!

The mystery of the missing shoes was solved and it had just cemented back the bond between the brothers.

Misunderstandings are common amongst brothers and friends over issues, big and small. Cool headedness and large heartedness often succeed in solving the issues.

48

The Only Cow

"Do not try to bring down the Almighty to your limited vision. Rise up, strengthen your detachment and establish yourself in discrimination, then your goal is brought nearer."

500
1000

In a village there were two farmers. One of them was rich and had hundreds of cows. He would sell milk to many people in the nearby city. The other one was poor and had only one cow. He spent most of his time looking after the cow, collecting fresh hay for it, milking it etc.

One day God and an Angel happened to cross by that village. They noticed that both the farmers were deeply engrossed in meditation and prayer. The Angel said, "Oh Benevolent one! Bless these two pious souls for they are so devoted to you!" God said, "I bless them both."

The rich farmer suddenly became richer. His cows gave double the milk, they used to and his fortune just multiplied. But the poor farmer's only cow, died the next day.

The Angel was flabbergasted. He asked God, "Oh Merciful one! The fortune of the rich farmer is increasing by leaps and bounds, but what about this poor man? Do you see how bitterly he is crying? What will he do without his beloved cow? How will he fend for himself?"

God smiled, "My dearest one! Listen to me. The rich farmer has yet to go through the cycle of birth and death many times. He needs all the wealth he has and more, to live a comfortable life. This poor man is just about ready to merge with me. He has persevered towards Moksha over many births. The only obstacle in his way was his attachment to his cow. So I have taken it away. Now he is ready to be one with me! Don't be sorry for him, I know what is best for him."

God always knows what is best for us. How so ever much we think we know; He always knows best.

Baba tells us, "Everyone has to achieve moksha (liberation), whether one is striving for it now or not. It is the inevitable end to the struggle, the goal to which all are proceeding. But, please do not be afraid of reaching the goal of liberation. Well, how do you prepare yourself for the stage? The answer is in that very word Moksha, itself. It is self-explanatory. 'Mo' indicates Moha, that is delusion or being deluded by attractive but transitory trash; and 'ksha' stands for kshaya, disappearance or decline. In other words, to attain liberation one must keep the flights of your mind away from these deluding attractions, and focus on the straight path towards liberation."

49
The Burning Cat

"Can the results justify the means? Fair ends through foul means can never be right."

An old man died leaving behind four sons. They divided all his property and valuables equally. After everything was accounted for, a pet cat that the old man loved dearly was left. The question before them was how to divide the cat. Eventually it was decided that all four of them would look after it. Each of its legs was allocated to one of the sons. Each of them was to take up the responsibility of feeding the cat once, at four different times of the day.

The cat became a VIP and was absolutely pampered. One day the cat hurt one of its legs. So one of the brothers who was the designated owner of that leg, took the cat to a vet and got a bandage done. The next day all the four brothers were away to work and the cat was limping around the house. Its foot happened to brush across a burning oil lamp. Its bandage being oily caught fire. The frightened cat ran helter-shelter with its burning leg, all over the house. It ran up the sofas, across the curtains, into the kitchen and the bed rooms crying desperately for help. But there was no one around to help the miserable creature.

With its burning limb, the cat managed to spread the fire to many pieces of furniture and finally the whole house caught fire. The cat just managed to run out of the door in agony.

When the brothers returned home they were devastated to see the cat crying piteously and the whole house up in flames!

The brother, who owned the injured leg, nursed the cat while he wept over the loss of the house. The other three brothers blamed the fourth one saying that it was because the bandaged leg had caught fire that this misfortune had befallen them. So the owner of the bandaged leg should pay up and compensate for the loss of the other three.

The brothers got into a bitter quarrel and no solution seemed to be forthcoming. So they took the matter to the king. The king heard them out and realized that it was really not any body's fault. But whatever had happened; had happened! The other three brothers were being quite unreasonable in putting all the blame on the fourth brother who was the owner of the injured leg. The king said, “It seems that the injured leg caught fire and the cat ran from pillar to post looking for help. But it could not have run around on its injured leg because it would have been very painful being hurt as well as burning. The other three healthy legs 'ran' from here to there, thereby causing the fire to spread. So the cause of the inferno is the three healthy legs and not the injured leg. You three brothers should pay compensation to the fourth one!”

All things cannot always be divided amongst children. Parents always remain equally inclined towards all their off springs and it is futile to try and divide their love.

50

Little Fire Brigade

"Be helpful to others; then your conscience itself will appreciate you and keep you happy and content, though others may not thank you."

FIRE
BRIGADE
FIRE

A fire was raging in a little hut near the bank of a river. Several people were running to and fro filling buckets from the river and throwing them into the fire in an effort to douse it. Two small children were crying seeing their house go up in flames. A tiny bird filled her beak with water and flew over the towering inferno and let the water drop into it. The scorching heat singed her wings but that did not deter her from her mission. Valiantly she flew back to the river to fill more water in her tiny beak and flew back again to spit out the water over the fire. She continued to make these trips to the river to bring water from the river, as tediously as the people who were toiling with their buckets. The entire team worked frantically while a lazy crow sat atop a tree and watched the tumultuous scene below. The crow called out to the little bird saying, "Hey birdie, why are you wasting your time? Your tiny beak barely holds a drop or two of water in it. What can that do to put the fire out?"

The bird replied panting, "Howsoever small the amount of water may be, at least it is something. And something is better than nothing!" The crow scoffed at her saying, "These people haven't been able to douse the fire with their buckets full of water. What can you do with your tiny droplets? Hah! You're just wasting your time. Come sit by me and rest your tired wings!"

The bird persisted in its efforts to play 'fire brigade' and the crow continued to ridicule her. Finally the bird stopped and said, "My contribution may be miniscule, but when the history of this event is written, my name shall be quoted amongst those who helped in putting the fire out; neither amongst those who started it nor with those who chose to sit around and did nothing else but criticize!"

Sitting around and passing idle comments is very easy. It is not everyone who can feel the pain of another deep enough to get up and render help. Most of us would see the fire from afar and say, "Uh ho! What a terrible fire." That's it! And we would just go our way! How many of us would stop to help?

When somebody is sad, do you feel the pain in your heart? Do you ever try and offer comfort or solace to a distraught stranger? Everyone loves their own people. If you can love others for no reason at all and with no expectation of return, that is what makes you different.

51

"Why Today?"

"One's body is derived from the flesh and blood of the mother. How much sacrifice is involved in giving birth to a child and rearing that child with continuous care and love is beyond description."

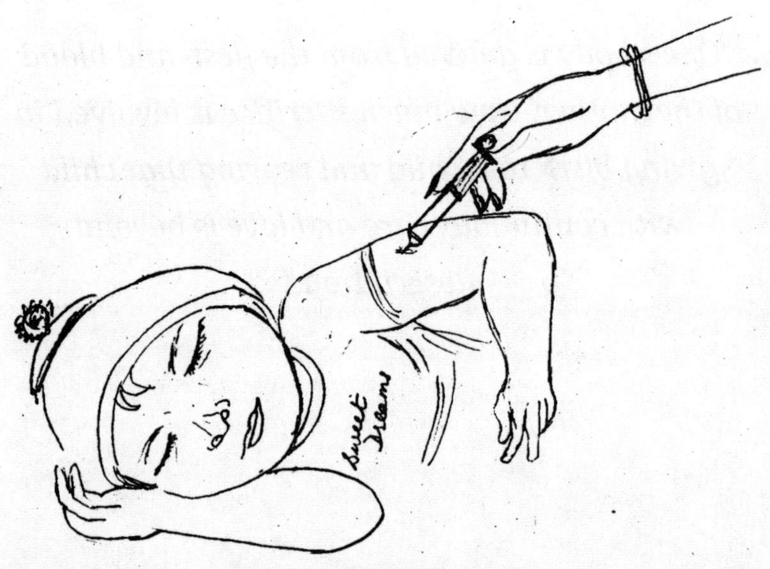
Sweet Dreams

Aprangi was on her way to work. Despite it being early morning, she was terribly late for work. The streets were strewn with autumn leaves. There had been a slight drizzle in the night. Some of the drains were water logged and puddles of water were inconveniencing the pedestrians. But work is work and the clock was ticking fast. Aprangi walked as fast as she could, trying her best to avoid the slush and the muck on the road.

Oops! In the haste, her foot slipped on a rotting leaf and she fell on the road. Her hands were bruised and dirty. Her knees were obviously bleeding, going by the torn salwar and the fast spreading blood stain. Slowly she got up. Thankfully there were no bones broken. But she cursed under her breath. "Why today, of all days ... when I'm already late." Her suit was all soiled by the muddy water; she couldn't possibly go to work in this state. Her boss's angry and haughty face flashed before her mind and she cringed in discomfort. With a lot of effort she limped to the next crossing and managed to get an autorikshaw guy to stop, "10, Kishan Road," she said.

Once in the auto, she opened her purse, to get her cell phone out and call her office to inform that she would be late. The cell was missing and she realized that she had left it at home, "Why today, of all days ..." she cursed. Hurriedly, she entered home. She was surprised to see the maid servant, giving a syrup to her five month old baby boy. The bottle was in the maid's hand and the baby had just finished licking the sweet cherry flavoured concoction. She grabbed the bottle from the maid. The ground slipped from under her feet as she read the label to realize that it was a strong sedative. A rapid fire of questions revealed that the maid had been sedating the child for over a month. The baby was blissfully in deep sleep.

Aprangi realized why the baby boy had been so playful all night for the past month or so. He had obviously been sleeping all day. So he would refuse to sleep at night.

With tears in her eyes she tucked the baby into bed. As the blood from her bruised palms stained the sheet, she remembered why she had come home in the first place. She then cleaned her wounds, bandaged them and put on fresh clothes.

Aprangi remembered what she had said a short while back, "Why today, of all days!" Then it dawned on her, if she had not fallen and hurt herself, she would not have come back home. If she had not come home at that inopportune moment, she would not have caught the maid doing what she was!

Sometimes, maybe you just need to fall down! Sometimes, maybe you just need to get hurt! Sometimes, may be that is the only way for God to make you see things that you are otherwise blind too!

Everything happens for a reason. Everything happens by the will of God. Sometimes; or rather most of the times; we wonder why things are going wrong. Trust in God, He has His own ways.

52

Vidya!

"True education means trying to manifest the inner divinity in man. How is this manifestation to be brought about? Students must receive education that illumines every aspect of life - the economic, the political, the moral, the spiritual and the physical, the mental and the social environment of man. It should not be confined to one specific sphere. Many students consider book knowledge as education. This gives them only superficial knowledge. They need practical knowledge which will enable them to lead righteous lives."

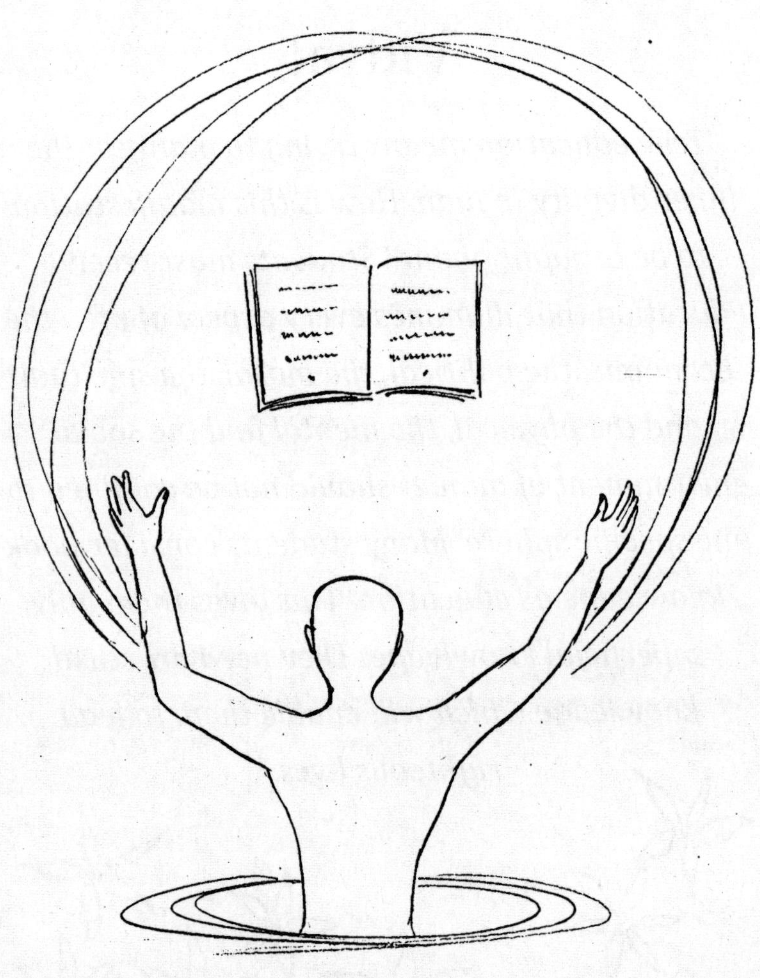

A young disciple having spent many years with his Guru, asked him a question, "Sir, I have acquired so much knowledge on all the subjects during my stay here. But I am not at peace. Tell me, which Vidya is that which leads to complete knowledge of everything there is to know in the universe.

The Guru was pleased at the disciple. He said, "This is such a simple question. Yet the most fundamental and pertinent! Let me explain. There are two types of education. Para and Apara. Apara Vidya includes all that can be acquired through education, about all the subjects you can think of. It includes languages, literature, science, technology, geography ... including all the sacred texts."

"Para Vidya is the knowledge gained through the process and progress while traversing from I to we; from Atma to Paramatma. The transformation and evolution is what Para Vidya is all about.

Apara vidya is limited to knowledge. Para Vidya is about understanding through experience. Talking about understanding through experience, the ancients tell us about Divya drishti. Drishti literally means sight. Most of us have eyes, so we have sight. Some of us have foresight and some are farsighted while others can see only in hindsight! Same may have insight too ... A combination of insight and foresight may result in vision. A person with a vision or a visionary may not necessarily be physically sighted. He may even be physically blind. Remember Soordas!

When vision is directed by devotion to the Divine in the form of

Bhakti and insight is evolved enough to attain Viveka, a person may acquire Divya Drishti!

On a mundane level, the modern system of education talks only about attainment of knowledge. Sadly the modern student learns the text, only with a view to pass the exam. The understanding is not the focus and experience is absolutely far-fetched, because in the fast pace of life, we want to achieve so much in such little time. When multi-tasking is the order of the day, understanding just gets left behind somewhere. At junior school, when our generation was taught 3x6=18 it meant that, if I had 3 chocolates each in a pack and had 6 packs, or conversely if I had 3 packs containing 6 chocolates each; I had altogether 18 chocolates. It also meant that 3+3+3+3+3+3=18. But today's child is in too much of a hurry. He just picks up the calculator and punches 3x6=18. He may not understand how he arrived at the number 18.
Just theoretical knowledge may create clutter in the mind. The mind has to be stilled, in order that it may think, pause, wonder and ruminate ...With each passing day we learn new things. Learning and experience are never ending. Have you ever wondered what the last thing one learns by experience is? It is the experience of dying!

Complete education cannot be attained by just attending classes and clearing exams ... the experience of life is an education at every moment. The human mind is so fickle and wavering in nature that many of us go through life without understanding the purpose or the value of life. It is only the blessed few that experience the bliss of having connected with the Divine and understanding the 'why' of life!

Thanksgiving

We thank you swami!
... for letting us be a part of you and
... for choosing us to work for you.

We thank you Swami!
... for each little thought that you send
... towards the completion of this end.

We thank you Swami!
... for keeping us close and safe and
... for holding us in your eternal embrace.

We thank you Swami!
... for being to us a mother and a father
... such that in the world we have to look no further.

- Priya and Sanjay Tandon

Excerpts from some letters received by us:

I have read those wonderful stories, some of which I knew earlier. You have done a very commendable job indeed by publishing them in a book form. I have the similar feelings as expressed by Smt Sushma Swaraj in her foreword and by Shri Kaw in his 'wishes'. The book is unputdownable, and holds us till the last and makes us ask for more! I am also fond of tales and anecdotes. Generally, many of the Sangh adhikaris invariably employ tales and anecdotes in their bouddhiks. I was hugely benefited by our meeting! Hope to hear from you more. Anyhow you have found a wonderful means to keep in touch- daily thought and weekly story!
Thanks a lot. Kindly extend my namaskars to Smt Priya Tandon who is an indivisible part of your mission. In fact wherever I have said "you" above, it means both ' Smt Priya and Shri Sanjay'. ***- Best wishes, Datta Hosabale***

I have recently read your book 'Sunrays for Sunday'. And your stories bring tears to my eyes. My friend gifted this book long back and I never got the time to read it but today when he is no more with me, I don't know how but there was a feeling to read this book and when I completed it I understood that he wants me to be a better person and should know what my life purpose is. I am very thankful to you for showing me, and many others the right way of leading a good and spiritual life...though my spiritual journey has already started after my friend's death who taught me the truth of life but your book is like finding another GEM in this beautiful journey...keep up the good work. I m looking forward to read your other editions too... ***Loads of love, Sheenu***

This is the best thing to start your day with, I am receiving these thoughts for a long time now, whenever you read them you feel a positive effect on your way of thinking, they have given me strength through my difficult times, it feels as if Baba is so near to you and giving you directions not to lose heart, difficulties come and go ,don't ever be disheartened, I also have your collection of books, i.e Sunrays Series, awesome collection of stories from the life of normal people. Each story has such a meaning moral, and it has such a great impact on your way of thinking, after reading them your way of living your life changes completely, Thank you for bringing this positivity in my life. ... ***Priyanka Sabharwal***

My name is Ramesh Menon and I thought of congratulating both of you for bring out the Sunrays series. When I visited Dharmakshetra on last Saturday, Sep 3,2011. I received a SMS from my sister staying at Nerul asking me to buy the entire "Sunrays" series as one of her friends told her it was worth reading. Before handing over to her I decided to browse through the books and I really liked the compilation. Some of the stories I have already read elsewhere, all the same it was a nice experience to go through them once again. When I used to read Chicken Soup for the Soul and Small Miracle series, I used to wonder why can't our Indian authors with resources do something similar. And once again I thank and congratulate you for bring out these series. I have already started tweeting to my friends about this. With warm regards and with a prayer that May lord continue to shower His benign grace on you both and may that flow through you to others. Sairam. - ***Ramesh Menon***

Clarification

Sairam! This book has been written from the heart. Each story is preceded by a quote from the teachings of our beloved Bhagwan Sri Sathya Sai Baba. The flow of words and expressions is as downloaded from the divine vibrations resonating in the cosmos. Despite utmost care, if however any material has crept in that causes hurt to any person or community, we offer our unconditional apologies for the same. Many thoughts are based on what we have read on the internet, as have been shared by others. The common objective is to add value to the world in our endeavour to do our bit to make the world a better and happier place. Let's be each other's strength in the cause!!!

- Priya and Sanjay Tandon